Ultimate

ITALIAN

TRIVIA

Dedicated to my wife Christina

A Treasure Trove of
Fun and Fascinating Facts

SCOTT PAUL FRUSH

MARSHALL RAND PUBLISHING

Royal Oak, Michigan

Marshall Rand Publishing

P.O. Box 1849
Royal Oak, Michigan 48068

Printed in the United States of America

Although every precaution was made in preparation of this book, the publisher and author assume no responsibility for omissions or errors biographical or otherwise.

Frush, Scott P.
    Ultimate Italian trivia: a treasure trove of fun and fascinating facts / Scott P. Frush

ISBN 0-9744374-8-4

Library of Congress Control Number: 2004113545

CONTENTS

CHAPTERS

ACKNOWLEDGEMENTS

There are some very special people I would like to thank that helped make this book possible. First and foremost, thank you to my wife Christina for her heroic support for this project, her time in editing every trivia, and for allowing me to express my thoughts and ideas on this book almost daily. I could not have accomplished this Herculean feat without her assistance.

A very special thank you to Frank D. Stella for writing such a wonderful Foreword to this book. I am most appreciative for this and the guidance and suggestions he made throughout the project.

Thank you to Mario Fallone for his support and encouragement of this book. For some of the amazing photographs of Italy found in this book, I thank Edi and Maria Zanini and John and Heather Northcott.

Molto grazie to my friends at the National Italian American Foundation (www.niaf.org) for their generous financial support of this book. I am truly honored by their recognition.

Many thanks to my wonderful family and friends for their significant encouragement, generous assistance, and unwavering support. Their time and contributions are greatly appreciated.

- Scott Paul Frush

ABOUT THE AUTHOR

Scott Paul Frush received his masters degree from the University of Notre Dame and his bachelors degree from Eastern Michigan University. He also completed coursework at the University of Chicago.

Scott is president of Frush Financial Group, a Bloomfield Hills, Michigan based wealth management firm offering investment, tax, and insurance solutions.

Scott is an accomplished financial advisor, a noted investment author, publisher of the *Journal of Asset Allocation*, and proponent of Catholic values investing.

Scott with wife Christina at Saint Peter's Square, Vatican City

Prior to establishing his company, Scott worked at Jay A. Fishman Investment Counsel in Detroit and Stein Roe Mutual Funds in Chicago. He holds the Chartered Financial Analyst (CFA) and Certified Financial Planner (CFP®) designations.

Scott is a self-proclaimed history buff, trivia extraordinaire, Italian culture connoisseur, and avid writer. During his trip to Tuscany in 2004, he proposed to his wife Christina, the daughter of Italian immigrants from the town of Sant' Elia. Christina and he are parish members of Saint Hugo of the Hills Catholic Church.

Scott is a member of the National Italian American Foundation, the Order Sons of Italy in America, and the Italian American Club of Livonia (Michigan), where he and his wife are receiving Italian language instruction.

Scott is the author of three other books; *Understanding Asset Allocation* (McGraw-Hill, 2006); *Understanding Hedge Funds* (McGraw-Hill, 2007); and

Optimal Investing (Marshall Rand Publishing, 2004), the recipient of two *Book of the Year* honors for business and investments.

MORE FROM SCOTT PAUL FRUSH

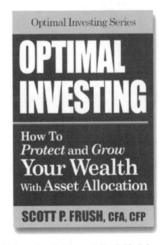

McGraw-Hill	Marshall Rand Publishing
2006	**2004**

► COMING EARLY 2007 ◄

Understanding Hedge Funds
By Scott Paul Frush and McGraw-Hill

These books are available online at www.ScottPaulFrush.com, www.Amazon.com, *or at your favorite local bookseller.*

LIST OF FEATURES

TOP 10 OF ITALY:

OTHER FEATURES:

FOREWORD

Ultimate Italian Trivia, by author Scott Paul Frush, demonstrates profound research and includes over a thousand superb trivia - some humorous and many intellectual - about Italian culture and way of life. Reading these interesting trivia questions makes you think how little one really knows about Italians and their culture. Moreover, as you read each trivia in this book, you will feel proud to be Italian or you will feel that you want to become part of this wonderful culture as the book covers so many diverse areas regarding Italian life, culture and people. *Ultimate Italian Trivia* is a book that every Italian American should have and read, including non-Italians who can use this book to compare and contrast their own nationality.

The fabulous regions of Italy, each uniquely different from one another, can be thought of as countries in their own regard. Their unique cuisine, cultural and social arts, sports, linguistic dialect, work habits, and spiritual quest are the best of Italy. Despite the profound differences throughout the regions, you will always find the people to be warm, hospitable, and proud of their Italian heritage; thus a profound beauty and spiritual awareness is eminent throughout the regions. Together with their lust for life, the people of Italy are the real treasurers. The attitude of one for all and all for one is alive and well in the Italian culture.

Italy is the center of the beautiful Mediterranean Sea, for centuries the seal of the Etruscan and Roman Empire - a fabulous and valiant part of Italian history. Together with many other Italian Americans, one can find his or her regional roots with the help of this book. *Ultimate Italian Trivia* spans the history of the Italians from the Etruscans to the Romans, from the Catholic Church to the Vatican and from the early wars to the modern wars and conflicts that Italians have participated in. This book helped me and reminded me of the great history of the Italians.

I am proud to write this foreword for its author, Scott Paul Frush. Although he is not Italian, and should be, he has a strong passion about the people, history, and culture of Italy. His passion is for everything Italian, including his wife Christina, the daughter of a good friend of mine, Mario Fallone. His writing is presently helping his Italian studies where he will soon speak fluent Italian as he and his wife are studying this beautiful language. I predict that he will be a profiled author about Italians and will be on the bestseller list!

The author, whose brilliant thoughts on writing *Ultimate Italian Trivia*, will be honored when the book becomes a bestseller. Then we, Italian Americans, can bestow upon him the signet of "Honorary Italian". Our and his beloved, National Italian American Foundation, can even suggest a name change – Scotti Paulo Frushi. We are proud of him. Please read this book and enjoy.

- Frank D. Stella
Detroit, Michigan

▶ *Frank D. Stella is chairman emeritus and active member of the National Italian American Foundation. Mr. Stella is chairman and CEO of The F. D. Stella Products Company, a Detroit-based company founded in 1946 that designs and distributes food service and dining equipment.*

Mr. Stella is an alumnus of the University of Detroit College of Commerce and Finance. He has served as a board member of the University of Detroit/Mercy, Wayne Community College Foundation, Mt. Carmel Mercy Hospital, Sacred Heart Rehabilitation Center, as well as the National Republican Committee, Michigan Finance Republican Committee and National Heritage Groups Council.

Mr. Stella was decorated by the government of Italy three times and received its highest decoration, "Grande Ufficiale". In 1997, he was selected Michigander of the year. Mr. Stella is an appointee of four United States presidents – Richard Nixon, Gerald Ford, Ronald Reagan and George Bush, Sr. ◀

INTRODUCTION

Ciao Amici!

"La Dolce Vita", the sweet life, an expression that stirs up emotions and conjures up visions of the eloquent Italian experience. Amore, espresso, famiglia, pasta, Rome, Tuscany, opera, vino. They are but a few of the extraordinary elements underlying the Italian experience. Each time you sip Chianti or dine on the delight of Tiramisu, you are enjoying the Italian legacy and what Italy has given to the world. The range of contributions to everyday life is truly astonishing.

Today we live in a world of remarkable invention and discovery. All cultures, past and present, have contributed to some degree and in some manner. However, those of Italian heritage have contributed to our world as much, if not more, than any other culture. The evidence is clear, unambiguous and far reaching. Italians have developed a remarkable tradition of passion, excellence and accomplishment that is the envy of much of the entire world. From the beginning of modern civilization to the invention of countless civilization "firsts", Italians have done it all. From the past to the present, the Italian culture is perhaps the richest and truly most inspiring of the entire world. This book intends to convey what is surly the best and most notable about Italians and their rich heritage and culture.

All of the major periods of Italian history are covered in ***Ultimate Italian Trivia***, including the Etruscans, the ancient Roman Empire, the Middle Ages, the Renaissance, the Holy Catholic Church, the unification (called in Italian the Risorgimento, or "Resurgence") and finally the modern era. Recreating and rediscovering the Italian experience was at the forefront of my drive while writing this book. In my judgment, this book is part travel guide, part cookbook, part Italian language guide, part science book and part business success guide. All things Italian wrapped into one.

Italians have been very instrumental in shaping of western civilization in so many ways. The breadth and depth of their influence is quite remarkable. Italians have given the world contributions in such fields as literature, politics, music, food, science, banking, language and invention. In addition, more than twenty six million Americans proudly trace their heritage to Italy. Among this group are very distinguished luminaries from the fields of business, sports, entertainment, politics and the arts. This book will help you to learn and understand many of their accomplishments and contributions.

Ultimate Italian Trivia covers a very broad spectrum of Italian trivia. This was done since people have very different interests and appreciation for different things. One person may be more interested in Italian cuisine and language while another may be more interested in Italian military history and scientific contributions. Furthermore, some people will find treasure in the details while others like a holistic approach. An interesting trivia may be fascinating to some, but not to others. In consequence, every effort was made to balance the trivia topics and provide for all particular interests. However, given the amount of information on each topic, the chapters in this book each vary in size. Some chapters, such as Italian Americans and Italian cuisine, are much larger than the other chapters. In all, there are 15 total chapters with 14 of those chapters dedicated to trivia questions. The final chapter is dedicated to the answers for all of the questions in the preceding 14 chapters. Finally, each chapter targets a specific subject and, as a result, presents trivia questions that are related. In addition to the 15 chapters, there are appendices with useful non-trivia information.

Appendix A provides a solid list of Italian American resources, including newspapers, magazines, and cultural centers. Appendix B provides a list of recent Italian statesmen, including the prime ministers, presidents and kings of Italy. Appendix C covers the Italian national anthem in both Italian and English, side-by-side. Finally, Appendix D provides useful profiles on each of the twenty regions of Italy.

Included in the chapters are photographs of Italy and featured content. This featured content includes "Top 10 of Italy" lists, "It Happened In..." event profiles, and a timeline of key dates in Italian history at the top of each page.

In his book, *Italians First*, author Arturo Barone said it best; "Above all, it is the Italian approach to life and style which creates the particular aura which appeals to so many." From the *Mona Lisa* to the Roman Colosseum and from the rolling hills of Tuscany to the snow-caped Dolomites of northern Italy, the Italian experience and approach to life and style will take your breath away.

Many people ask me how I was able to identify so many trivia, especially when I am not Italian. The answer is quite simple – I did a tremendous amount of research. I poured over dozens and dozens of books, researched every relevant website I could find, watched television programs in hopes of uncovering the diamond in the rough, subscribed to nearly a dozen Italian American newspapers and magazines, and became a student of observation when my wife and I attended Italian social events. Conducting the research and writing this book were without a doubt a lot of work, but well worth it all.

It is my sincere desire that ***Ultimate Italian Trivia*** becomes both your travel companion and historical reference guide. I've planted the seed of Italian discovery and exploration, now I turn it over to you for your reading enjoyment. So join me for a fun and fascinating journey through all things Italian...*Andiamo!*

- Scott Paul Frush
Royal Oak, Michigan

CHAPTER O·N·E

ASTRONOMY, EXPLORATION, & TRANSPORTATION

Italian Discoveries of New Worlds

"If we do not free and unite the whole of Italy, we shall never achieve liberty in any part of her."

- GIUSEPPE GARIBALDI

"I have not told half of what I saw."

- MARCO POLO

(1) On August 3, 1492 Christopher Columbus set sail with ninety sailors and three ships on his first voyage of discovery. Name his three ships.

(2) Born in Genoa around 1450, I am known for my service to the English crown and for claiming land that became the first American colonies. Who am I?

(3) According to an ordinance that dates back hundreds of years, how many colors can gondolas be painted?

(4) In Italy, what does the street sign "Senso Unico" signify?

(5) Christopher Columbus referred to this newly discovered food as "pinas de Indes", or Indian pine cone. What fruit did Columbus discover and bring back to Europe?

(6) In contrast to street addresses in the United States, how are street addresses typically written in Italy?

(7) This island, located due north of South America in the West Indies, was discovered by Columbus on his third voyage to the New World in 1498. What is the name of this island Columbus named for the Holy Trinity?

(8) What is the name for highways and expressways in Italy?

(9) Born in Florence around 1483, I am known for my great exploration of the North American coast. In addition, I was the first European to explore present-day New York harbor and the first to prove that the New World was indeed a new land and not part of Asia. Who am I?

(10) What do Cristobal Colon and Cristovio Colombo have in common?

(11) Measuring 36 feet long, weighing 1,323 pounds and having its port side (left) longer than its starboard side (right), this craft transports people through the streets of Venice. Name this craft that dates to A.D. 1094.

(12) What event motivated Queen Isabella and King Ferdinand to fund Christopher Columbus and his exploration to find a trade route to India and China?

(13) Which Italian explorer became the first European to set foot on the continent of South America?

(14) This present-day form of transportation was introduced by a 16th century Italian family that moved to Germany and founded a business of transporting items from one area to another. Shortly after arriving in Germany, the family changed their last name to the German version, "Taxis". What is this form of transportation?

(15) How many voyages of discovery did Christopher Columbus make to the New World?

(16) What is the name of the main airport in Rome?

(17) This person, the brother of a famous Italian explorer, founded in 1496 the oldest continuously inhabited city in the New World, Santo Domingo, and even modeled the design after a Roman grid fashion. Name this person.

(18) In 1493, Columbus made his second voyage of discovery. On this voyage, he sailed with seventeen ships and 1,500 sailors. Where did he explore?

(19) The city of Lyon was founded by the Romans in 43 B.C. as Lugdunum. In which present-day nation is this city located?

(20) Where did Christopher Columbus first make landfall in the New World on his maiden voyage in 1492, subsequently claiming the land for the King and Queen of Spain?

TOP 10 OF ITALY
Longest Rivers

	RIVER	DISTANCE	LOCATION
1	Po	652	Piedmont, Lombardy, Emilia-Romagna, Veneto
2	Adige	410	Trentino-Alto Adige, Veneto
3	Tevere	405	Emilia-Romagna, Tuscany, Umbria, Lazio
4	Adda	313	Lombardy
5	Oglio	280	Lombardy
6	Tanaro	276	Piedmont, Liguria
7	Ticino	248	Switzerland, Piedmont, Lombardy
8	Arno	241	Tuscany
9	Piave	220	Veneto
10	Reno	211	Tuscany, Emilia-Romagna

Distance in Kilometers

(21) What is a vaporetto?

(22) In Italy, which two words are used in pedestrian walk/do not walk street corner signs?

(23) When the Spanish are celebrating "Hispanic Day" and the people of the Bahamas are celebrating "Discovery Day", who are they honoring?

(24) John Cabot, born Giovanni Caboto, sailed under a foreign flag and claimed many parts of Canada for this nation. Which nation did he serve?

(25) How many places claim to have the human remains of Christopher Columbus?

(26) During the first century B.C., a Roman legion established a settlement called Liquiam in the Far East, the only one of its kind. In which present-day country was this distant settlement located?

(27) Which person introduced corn, tobacco, peppers and sweet potatoes to Italy and the rest of Europe?

(28) Which country in the Western Hemisphere is named after Italian explorer Christopher Columbus?

(29) This famous Italian luxury ocean liner sank off the American coast in 1956, with a loss of 46 lives, after colliding with another ship, the Stockholm. Name this Italian ship.

(30) Born in Florence in 1454, I am known for my great explorations of the New World. In 1507, German geographer Martin Waldseemuller published a map suggesting that the New World be named for me. Who am I?

> **IT HAPPENED IN...8000 B.C.**
>
> ▶ **The earliest known Paleolithic communities begin to develop in Italy, primarily in northern areas around Piedmont and Liguria.**

(31) In what language did Christopher Columbus record the accounts of his travels?

(32) During the 20th century, which two Latin American countries attracted the most Italian immigrants?

(33) Although Columbus discovered the New World, which Florentine explorer is credited with establishing that the discovery was not India or the Orient, but instead an undiscovered land?

(34) On order of the King of Naples, the first excavations of the buried city of Pompeii were commenced. In what century was the buried city finally rediscovered?

(35) What does a red sign with a yellow letter "M" signify in Italy?

(36) Discovered and named by Italian explorer Amerigo Vespucci, this country in the Western Hemisphere is named in honor of Venice. Name this country.

(37) This Italian explorer was the first person to claim that another ocean, perhaps even larger than the Atlantic Ocean, must exist beyond the New World. Name this explorer.

(38) This person, explorer of North America from North Carolina to Newfoundland, was the first European to explore New York and named the area Rhode Island. Name this Italian explorer born near Venice.

(39) The largest monument to Christopher Columbus can be found in which American city? (a) Newark (b) Baltimore (c) New York

(40) Which two Italian cities operate metro subway systems?

(41) Italian John Cabot, born Giovanni Caboto, discovered and claimed what land in the New World for England?

(42) Giovanni da Verrazano, the Italian explorer who sailed the eastern seaboard of America, named this stretch of land Cape Pallavicini after the legendary Italian military general. Soon afterward, the cape was renamed by English colonists. What is the present-day name for this cape? (Hint: New England)

(43) This Italian explorer from Venice brought back from China vast knowledge, including that on gunpowder, petroleum, and the effects of drugs on people. Who is he?

(44) Although short lived, Isabella was the first European settlement in the New World. Name the Italian explorer who founded this settlement in present-day Dominican Republic.

(45) This road, begun by Appius Claudius Caecus in 312 B.C., originally connected Rome to Capua before being lengthened to Brundisi. This road, originally known in its day as Regina Viarum, or Queen of the Roads, was the most important road leading to and from ancient Rome to the Adriatic. One of two columns marking the end of the road still stands in the Apulian city of Brundisi. Name this road.

(46) While in Italy, if you find yourself traveling on a "pendolino", on what specifically are you traveling?

(47) Born in Venice around 1252, I am most known for my great travel of discovery to China. I served the Khan, then ruler over China, for twenty years as the governor of the Chinese province of Yangchow. Who am I?

(48) We have all heard the celebrated expression, "All roads lead to Rome". At its height, the ancient Roman Empire had more than 53,000 miles of roads. When was the first recorded *paved* road built in Rome?

(49) Marco Polo published *Divisamen dou Monde* (*Description of the World*), a book many consider the first travel guide in history. His book provided the greatest amount of information on China until the 19th century. In which language did he write his book?

IT HAPPENED IN...753 B.C.

▶According to legend, the city of Rome is founded by brothers Remus and Romulus on seven hills near the banks of the Tiber river. This claim is supported by archaeological evidence that small villages began to flourish in the same area.

(50) Verrazano, the great Italian explorer, originally established a name for himself in which questionable profession?

(51) In Italy, which color are the street signs for highways and which color for main roads?

(52) Aside from seafaring, what early trade did Christopher Columbus have for a brief period of time while living in Spain?

CHAPTER T·W·O

CUISINE & CULINARY CONTRIBUTIONS

The Essence of Italian Food and Drink

"Life is a combination of magic and pasta."

- FEDERICO FELLINI

"You better cut the pizza in four pieces because I'm not hungry enough to eat six."

- YOGI BERRA

(53) This triangular shaped pastry is made of thin, layered flakes of dough, all wrapped around a moist and creamy filling, typically almond flavor. Name this popular pastry.

(54) This food, invented by an Italian monk around 610 A.D., is shaped to mimic the folded arms of praying children. It was invented for the purpose of giving children an inducement and reward for memorizing their prayers. Name this food.

(55) This region of Italy boasts some of the finest lobsters in all of Europe. From here, lobsters make their way too many dinner plates and are enjoyed throughout Europe. Name this region.

(56) This Italian sparkling wine, produced in the regions of Friuli-Venezia Giulia and Veneto, is made from a variety of late-ripening white grapes. Name this wine.

(57) The father of modern ice cream is a 15th century Italian architect from the city of Florence. Name this person.

(58) Many Italians like to put anisette or sambuca into what drinks?

(59) What is the name for the noontime meal eaten by Italians?

(60) This pastry of Sicilian origin is a tube of crisp, fried pastry dough filled with ricotta cheese and other ingredients; including nuts, dried fruits and chocolate chips. Name this pastry.

(61) What gives red grapes their distinctive color?

(62) In 1917, Achille Gaggia of Milan invented a high-pressure machine to replace the outdated steam machine. This invention, even more popular today, produces a more flavorful and intense drink while reducing the time needed to produce it. Name the drink this machine produces.

(63) This type of mushroom, considered a delicacy in Italy, was described as "the Mozart of mushrooms" by Italian composer Rossini. Name this type of mushroom that primarily grows only near the towns of Asti and Alba.

(64) Rice is a very common ingredient of Italian cuisine. However, this was not always the case. Name the ethnic group that introduced rice to Italy, specifically Sicily.

TOP 10 OF ITALY
Tallest Mountains

	MOUNTAIN	HEIGHT	LOCATION
1	Mont Blanc	4,810	Valle d'Aosta
2	Mount Rosa	4,634	Piedmont / Valle d'Aosta
3	Cervino	4,478	Valle d'Aosta
4	Gran Paradiso	4,061	Piedmont / Valle d'Aosta
5	Pizzo Zupo	3,996	Lombardy
6	Ortles	3,899	Trentino-Alto Adige
7	Monviso	3,841	Piedmont
8	Mount Cevedale	3,764	Lombardy / Trentino-Alto Adige
9	Palla Bianca	3,738	Trentino-Alto Adige
10	Marmolada	3,342	Trentino-Alto Adige / Veneto

Height in Kilometers

(65) What desert shaped like a cone did Italo Marcioni create in 1896?

(66) Which Italian region was the first to embrace chocolate and even had recipes classified as state secrets?

(67) This Italian dish means "before the meal". Furthermore, this dish is typically served to not keep guests waiting for food and is usually served before the pasta course. Name this dish.

(68) How does Lasagna differ from the north to south of Italy?

(69) This type of bean was originally considered fodder for cattle in Sicily. However, people resorted to eating these beans during a severe famine that hit the area. Today, this bean symbolizes the intercession of Saint Joseph to the Almighty Father on our behalf. Name this type of bean.

(70) What is "sorbetto al melone"?

(71) What type of food is ricotta?

(72) This Italian desert, originating from Venice, is made of angel food cake, mascarpone cheese, liqueur and some combination of espresso or chocolate. The name of this desert literally translates to "pick-me-up" and was once thought to revive sexual vitology. Name this desert.

(73) Wines from this Italian region are widely used for blending and enhancing wines from other regions due to their high alcohol content, body, and nature. Name the region from which these wines originate.

(74) The first pasta factory in the United States was opened in 1848 by Frenchman Antoine Zerega. Where was this factory located?

(75) The word vermicelli, a type of pasta, translates to what in Italian?

(76) "Vino da tavola" is what type of drink?

(77) What does the word spaghetti mean in Italian?

(78) What is commonly referred to as "café americano" or "espresso lungo"?

(79) What popular liqueur, made from bitter almonds, was created in the early 16th century by a widow as a gift to artist Bernadino?

(80) This food product is made from the skin and pulp (musts) of crushed grapes. The musts are heated, aged and stored for long periods of time, typically twelve years or longer. Some extra vecchio brands can be aged for an entire century. Name this food product.

(81) Risotto is very popular in the city of Milan, often eaten in place of pasta. What exactly is risotto?

IT HAPPENED IN...69 A.D.

▶ Roman legions under the command of General Titus Flavius Vespasianus and his son Titus sack Jerusalem and destroy the Jewish Temple. Treasures from the Jewish Temple are brought back to Rome to pay for the building of the mighty Colosseum.

(82) What legendary Abruzzese meal begins at midday and frequently continues late into the night?

(83) What is the Italian term for perfectly cooked pasta?

(84) This food is icier, more flavorful, and denser than its American counterpart. In addition, this food has less air injected during production and is made with milk, not cream. Name this food that is the counterpart to ice cream.

(85) What type of red wine is considered the most important product of Verona?

(86) What is the name of the popular bitter vegetable commonly used in salad?

(87) If you see a restaurant advertising itself as "Vera Cucina Italiana", what is the restaurant owner claiming?

(88) Which world-famous chocolate brand was started by an Italian immigrant to the United States?

(89) How is authentic Napoletana pizza crust cooked?

(90) What did the ancient Romans add to wine before drinking?

(91) To protect the authenticity of true balsamic vinegar, Italian law prohibits the use of the word balsamic and reference to two provinces where authentic

balsamic vinegar is made, if not actually the case. In which two provinces in northern Italy is true balsamic vinegar produced?

(92) What is the name of the Christmas cake, originating from Siena, made of flour, cocoa, almonds, hazelnuts, spices and fruit?

(93) Prior to the 18th century, pizza was looked upon as what type of food in Italy?

(94) What grape is used to produce the Italian red wine Barbaresco?

(95) Due to availability and cost, this form of meat was rarely eaten by Italians in Italy many years ago. However, when Italians immigrated to America, where beef was plentiful and social workers recommended meat, they incorporated more meat into their cooking and thus gave birth to this form of meat. What did Italian Americans introduce?

(96) The name for this type of pasta means small tongues. Name this pasta.

(97) Although tomatoes originated from the Americas, what unique spin did Italians add?

(98) After what are sardines named?

(99) Venetian cuisine is known for their use of this type of food, considered an essential staple of their diet. Name this type of food.

(100) A Harvey Wallbanger drink consists of which Italian liqueur?

(101) Authentic Napoletana pizza has a paper-thin crust. Conversely, name the pizza with a thick, bready crust that Americans call Chicago-style deep dish.

(102) In the 18th century, pizza makers from Naples added what now common ingredient to pizza?

(103) Where is pasta, made with apple and brandy, a popular dish?

(104) Following his victory over Napoleon at the Battle of the Nile, British Admiral Nelson ordered vast quantities of what sweet Italian wine from Sicily to celebrate?

(105) Florentine Catherine de' Medici, bride of the French King, introduced what type of steak to France that is still enjoyed around the world today?

(106) Espresso is typically made from what type of coffee bean?

(107) What baking machine is used to create a thin checkerboard cookie?

(108) Name the town in Italy, known for its sparkling wine, which is home too much of the world's supply of white truffles.

(109) Olive trees are not native to Italy. From where did they originate?

(110) This tricolor pizza, created by Raffaele Esposito Brandi of Naples in honor of Queen Margherita of Savoy, is topped with mozzarella, tomatoes, and basil. The colors of the pizza represent the colors of the Italian flag. Name this type of pizza.

(111) People from Tuscany call this popular food "schiacciata" while people in northern Italy they call this food "focaccia". What is the more common name for this food?

(112) What group of people introduced pizza, a food that became popular overnight, to Americans in the mid-20th century?

(113) Italy is the world's largest producer of what type of drink?

(114) Americans consume over 12.5 million gallons (and climbing) of this food product each year. Name this food product that is a critical element of Italian cooking and cuisine.

(115) Studies show that two glasses of this drink per day helps to prevent diseases like Alzheimer's and Parkinson's. What is this drink?

(116) If you were served pancetta, what would you be eating?

(117) In which southern Italian region can you still find gigantic loaves of bread, with some toping twenty pounds?

(118) When someone uses the word "casalinga", to what are they referring?

(119) Caesar Cardini is credited with introducing what type of food dish that is traditionally eaten near the end of an Italian meal?

(120) What is the only utensil Italians use to eat pasta?

(121) Coffee was the rage of Italy during the 18th century, especially in Venice. By the middle of the 18th century, how many coffee houses did Venice alone have in operation?

(122) What does the Italian proverb, "a tavola non si invecchia", mean in English?

(123) In which city was mozzarella first added to pizza?

(124) In which Italian city did the pasta dish ravioli originate?

(125) This drink, a strong digestive liqueur flavored with herbs, is recognizable for its emerald green color. Name this drink.

(126) In Italy, if you were served "pulpo", what have you been given?

(127) What is the vegetable foundation of Alla Florentine?

(128) What feature makes olive oil more ideal for cooking than other types of oil?

(129) Which type of Italian red wine was at one time referred to as "pizza wine"?

(130) When did the use of olive oil originate in Italy?

(131) What is the name of the traditional Tuscan dish consisting of wide egg noodles typically served with lamb or veal sauce?

(132) What type of gum would you be chewing if the flavor were "Tutti Frutti"?

TOP 10 OF ITALY
Largest Islands

	ISLAND	AREA	LOCATION
1	Sicily	25,426	Sicily
2	Sardinia	23,813	Sardinia
3	Elba	224	Tuscany
4	Sant'Antioco	109	Sardinia
5	Pantelleria	83	Sicily
6	San Pietro	51	Sardinia
7	Asinara	51	Sardinia
8	Ischia	46	Campania
9	Lipari	37	Sicily
10	Salina	26	Sicily

Area is in Square Kilometers

(133) Bacala, or Pesce Stocco, is an Italian dish that uses either stockfish or sun dried fish. What variety of sun dried fish does it include?

(134) Zamponi is a popular food served in Italy. What exactly is zamponi?

(135) For what type of food were quality standards established by the pope in the 13th century?

(136) What is the primary difference between Italian and French bread?

(137) If you were served "il vino della casa", what exactly were you served?

(138) What does "cappelli di prete", a type of pasta, translate literally to in English?

(139) This food is a staple of the Italian diet, especially in Lombardy where it is served in place of pasta and risotto. Originating in Venice during the 16th century, this food resembles cornmeal mush and became popular after Columbus brought back corn to Europe. Name this food.

IT HAPPENED IN...64 A.D.

▶**Roman Emperor Nero burns part of Rome with the aim of clearing sections to rebuild on a grand scale. The setting of the fire is blamed on the Christians, who are subsequently rounded up and executed.**

(140) From where was the flat bread used in pizza most likely introduced?

(141) What is the name of the semi-hollow bread, served with lots of butter, that Milanese enjoy eating in the morning with café?

(142) For what is the town of Gorgonzola, located near Milan, most famous?

(143) Where and when did the first coffeehouse open in Italy?

(144) What type of cooking fat, originally only used to grease bodies before competition and battle, was added to Roman cuisine after Julius Caesar ate and liked it?

(145) Trenette is a type of pasta made without eggs that is typically combined with a traditional pesto sauce. Name the region from which this dish originates.

(146) This food, popular during Christmas, is a feathery golden yeast cake studded with citron and raisins. It is considered a traditional loaf of Italy with Milanese origins. Name this food.

(147) Ice cream can trace its origin to what treat eaten during ancient Roman times?

(148) Cow's milk has a fat content of 3.5%. What is the fat content of buffalo's milk used to make traditional mozzarella?

(149) Milanese cuisine is typically colored with which herb?

(150) What is the name for thin slices of toasted bread served with olive oil and herbs?

(151) What pear-shaped Emilian delicacy resembles ham, but is spicier with a stronger aroma?

(152) Real mozzarella is made with what type of milk?

(153) If you were dining on delicious "insalata di mare", what specifically were you eating?

(154) Vintage is very important with wine. What is the Italian word for vintage?

(155) What occupation is a cameriere?

(156) During what part of the day are cappuccinos and espressos traditionally enjoyed in Italy?

(157) How was Chianti wine bottled many years ago?

(158) Which fortified wine from Piedmont is flavored with aromatic herbs?

(159) When picking olives, which essential rule must be followed to ensure the olives do not become rancid and acidic?

(160) This vegetable - a form of chicory - is very popular in northern Italian salads and becoming popular in America under the name radicchio rosso. Name this vegetable.

(161) Traditionally, in what bodily position do Italians drink their café?

(162) What is a carafe?

(163) What is a demitasse?

(164) This dish consists of a slice of tomato sprinkled with olive oil and basil and toped with a generous slice of mozzarella cheese. Name this dish that originates from the Isle of Capri.

(165) If someone served you "vermicelli alle vongolo", what would you find mixed with the pasta?

(166) What is traditionally the last dish served during Italian meals?

(167) Which Italian family invented a popular vegetable, bearing their family name, by crossing cauliflower with Italian rabe?

(168) How did the drink cappuccino get its name?

(169) Lasagna can be traced to the ancient Roman era. Today, according to many, which two cities create the most authentic versions of Lasagna?

(170) What is "Granduca Cortese Di Gavi"?

(171) A bigolo is a hand extrusion machine used for making an essential food of the Italian cuisine. What food does the bigolo produce?

(172) If you see the words "al forno" after a food dish listed in a menu, what does this indicate about how the dish was cooked?

(173) What are the two best selling types of liquor in Italy?

(174) When an Italian asks for birra, for what is he requesting?

(175) What is the name of the famous Italian pudding from Piedmont?

(176) Which Italian gelato consists of three flavors, each with its own color wedge to represent a color on the Italian flag?

(177) Which traditional sauce, made of sweet basil, pine nuts, garlic olive oil and ewe's milk cheese, is an invention of Genoa?

(178) In which Italian city were boiled candies invented?

(179) This person, previously called an espresso puller, is an expert in the art of making espresso and espresso based drinks. What is the present-day name for this person?

(180) Although quite subjective, which Italian wine is considered by connoisseurs to be the finest wine in Italy?

(181) What is an Italian gelateria?

(182) What are the two most popular drinks in Italy?

(183) When Italians ask for coffee, for what specific drink are they requesting?

(184) What is meant by the expression "Si mangia bene in Bologna"?

(185) The ancient Etruscan and ancient Roman civilizations differed in so many ways. How did they differ in respect to the company at the dinner table?

(186) Francesco Procopio dei Coltelli established a chain of coffeehouses throughout Europe and in 1675 began to sell a type of desert food at his Café Procope in Paris, quickly becoming an instant success. Name this wildly popular desert.

(187) If you were served acqua del rubinetto for a drink in Italy, what were you given?

(188) What are the two types of Parmesan (Parmigiano) cheese?

(189) What is the English translation for mostarda?

(190) Struffoli is a traditional holiday food in Italy. What is struffoli?

(191) What is the most popular spice, symbolizing love and fertility, in Italy?

(192) This type of lean cured meat is a favorite of Piedmont and Lombardy. It is commonly eaten in paper-thin slices with extra-virgin olive oil, lemon juice, freshly ground black pepper, and freshly grated Parmigiamo. Name this food.

(193) People in the region of Apulia are known for their large appetite for pasta and their fondness for shellfish. Name the type of shellfish they are especially fond of eating.

(194) What is gnocchi di patate?

(195) When Italians ask for caffe corretto, for which type of drink are they asking?

(196) Frizzante is a fizzy type of water, while naturale is water without fiz. What then is ferrarelle?

(197) What does it mean when a dish is served Alla Parmigianino?

(198) Evidence shows that pasta was invented by what people in Italy around the 4th century B.C.?

(199) Which Italian food product must have less than 1% acidity by law?

(200) This drink is a type of brandy distilled from the pulpy mass combination of pits, skins and stalks remaining in a wine press after the juice of the grapes is extracted during wine making. Name this drink.

(201) A pizzelle most closely resembles what American breakfast food item?

(202) Referred to as the golden city of Umbria, this city in central Italy is noted for baking notoriously delicious chocolates. Name this city.

(203) This type of vegetable, introduced to France in the 16th century by Catherine de' Medici, originated in Sicily. This vegetable is grown in the sunniest areas of Italy and the varieties include small ones with spiny leaves and larger round-leaf ones known as "Roman". Name this vegetable.

(204) What is the name for the long dry cookie, typically dipped in coffee or wine and then eaten, made with either chocolates or almonds?

(205) Which type of fruit tree, now commonplace in Italy, did Roman General Lucullus import to Italy and Europe from Asia Minor in 79 B.C.?

(206) Three coffee beans are typically added to a drink of sambucca. What do they symbolize?

(207) What type of pasta was named to honor the Italian conquest of Tripoli in Libya?

(208) During the 16th century, which Italian city was the first to import coffee from North Africa and introduce it to both Italy and the rest of Europe?

(209) Wine labels imprinted with the phrase "Denominazione della Origine Controllata", or DOC, is a sign of what?

(210) If you want spaghetti sauce with meat, for what should you request?

(211) The tarecco blood orange has a red blush and thin skin. This orange is appreciated for its sweetness and is considered one of the world's best oranges. Where in Italy does the tarecco blood orange grow?

(212) What is the name for the cookies shaped to resemble knights and saints that are made in Calabria?

(213) What is the name of the rich and spongy Easter cake made in Sicily?

(214) The traditional pizza of Genoa is made with black olives, garlic and a generous dose of another topping. What is this topping?

(215) This area of Tuscany, arguably its most popular wine region, is said to be the world's oldest officially defined wine-growing region in Italy. Name this wine region established by Cosimo de' Medici.

(216) This fried and sweetened pastry puff, originating from Naples, is typically served on Saint Joseph's Day throughout southern Italy. Name this pastry.

(217) What is a taralli?

(218) Why is extra virgin olive oil considered higher quality than virgin olive oil?

(219) What is a frittata?

(220) Pomodoro is the Italian name for what well-known fruit that is nicknamed the "golden apple"?

(221) Pepper is one of the two most popular spices of northern Italian cooking. The other is "noce moscata", which means perfumed walnut. What is the more popular name for this second spice?

(222) What claim to fame does the Barilla pasta factory in Pedrignano, Italy boast?

(223) Which popular Italian soup is made with a variety of vegetables combined into a broth base of soup?

(224) What classification of tree is an olive tree?

(225) Some suggest that spaghetti originated in China and was introduced to Italy by Marco Polo. However, strong evidence counters this age-old claim. What is this evidence?

(226) What are the four key factors for making good espresso?

(227) Why did Italy not use tomatoes in their cooking until the 18th century?

(228) What are melanzane ripieni?

(229) Although this food - technically a fruit - is extremely popular in Italy, the soup made from it is not eaten in Italy. Name this food.

CHAPTER
T·H·R·E·E
III

ECONOMICS, MONEY, & BUSINESS

The Rise of Italian Commerce and Wealth

"Money to get power, power to protect money."

- MEDICI FAMILY MOTTO

"We are continually faced with great opportunities brilliantly disguised as insoluble problems."

- LEE IACOCCA

25

(230) This company, the top selling automaker in Italy, was founded in 1899, four years before the Ford Motor Company was founded by Henry Ford in 1903. Name this company.

(231) What famous cruise line, typically staffed by Italians, is headquartered in Genoa and promotes an Italian cruising experience?

(232) Florentines were the first to issue this type of insurance policy in the early 14th century to protect the cargos of ocean going vessels. Name this type of insurance policy.

(233) Which two nations are the leading importers to Italy? (Hint: both European)

(234) This present-day word originated from bankers who set up business in the streets of Florence and Siena by sitting behind benches, called bancos. Name this word, now used to describe an essential financial institution.

(235) What were the two names given to gold coins minted in Venice and in Florence during the Renaissance?

(236) What does the word Fiat, the automaker nameplate, stand for and mean?

(237) What type of fabric was made exclusively in Italy before the 17th century?

(238) Which two countries supply Italy with approximately 65% of all natural gas imports?

(239) Which company is Italy's largest single employer?

(240) What is Italy's top level Internet domain (e.g. .com and .net)?

(241) What type of shop in Italy has a characteristic white sign with a letter "T"?

(242) What was the "Battle for Grain"?

(243) In which Italian city was the oldest bank in the world, Banca Monte Paschi, founded in 1472?

(244) The art of shoemaking began in which Italian city in the 12th century?

(245) The modern banking system, as we know it today, was established and advanced by Italian Jews during the Renaissance. In which region did the foundation for modern banking thus originate?

(246) Only recently discovered in Spain, what unique map is now on display in the city of Turin?

(247) What financial instrument did the Bank of Venice invent in 1171 to facilitate purchases of personal and business property?

(248) This Italian sports automaker, acquired by Volkswagen subsidiary Audi, is recognized for their sleek and innovative body styles. Name this company. (Hint: Countach and Diablo)

(249) Textile manufacturing is Italy's second largest manufacturing industry. What is the largest manufacturing industry in Italy?

(250) What type of coin did Florence mint in 1252 that made this coin the first of this type in the world?

(251) Located in the financial center of London, England, this major street was established by Italian bankers from Lombardi. Name this street that is a counterpart to Wall Street in New York.

(252) Italy has scarce mineral resources, except for one found extensively in Tuscany. Name this mineral where Italy is the world's largest producer.

(253) What type of vehicle is a Ducati?

(254) Italy was the first European nation to mint what type of currency in 1998?

(255) What is the primary source of domestic energy generation in Italy?

(256) Which European nation is the leading destination for Italian exports?

(257) The concept of the personal check to pay bills originated in which city during the Renaissance?

(258) Approximately what percentage of the Italian economy, according to estimates, is attributed to underground business and activities that for the most part goes officially unreported?

(259) Name the top three luxury sports car manufactures in Italy.

(260) What is the estimated economic GDP impact to Italy from hosting the 2006 Winter Olympics in Turin?

(261) Prior to essentially cornering the banking field, how did the Medici family of Florence originally become prosperous?

(262) More than half of the industrial production in Italy was concentrated in three regions during the Industrial Revolution of the 19th century. Name these three regions.

(263) What are the two leading beer brewers in Italy?

(264) The European market accounts for approximately what percentage of total Italian commerce? (a) 27% (b) 49% (c) 60%

(265) This company, where 49.9% of the stock is owned by the Italian government, is the national airline of Italy. Name this airline.

(266) What is the name for the very popular motor scooter seen on the streets of Italy?

(267) Approximately what percentage of Italy's energy requirements is imported from foreign sources? (a) 34% (b) 58% (c) 85%

(268) This symbol, "Il Cavallino Rosso", originated from the badge of a World War One Italian flying squadron. The badge was given to Enzo Ferrari by the father of an Italian fighter ace, Francesco Baracca, who had 36 kills. Ferrari places this symbol on each car they manufacturer. What is this symbol?

(269) In what year did Italy switch from using the Lira to using the Euro?

TOP 10 OF ITALY
Most Populated Cities

	CITY	POPULATION
1	Rome	2,553,873
2	Milan	1,299,439
3	Naples	995,171
4	Turin	902,255
5	Palermo	675,277
6	Genoa	605,084
7	Bologna	374,425
8	Florence	368,059
9	Bari	328,458
10	Catania	305,773

Population does not include metropolitan area

(270) Born in Rome in 1918, Franco Modigliani was the 1985 Nobel Laureate in Economics. What pioneering research did he achieve that led to this recognition?

(271) Which Italian city has the highest office rental rates? (a) Rome (b) Naples (c) Florence (d) Milan (e) Genoa

(272) What does the word "Alfa" in Alfa Romeo stand for and mean?

(273) Per person, what does Italy boast more of than any other nation in the world? (a) cars (b) scooters (c) telephones

(274) Although this statistic differs from region to region, what is the overall ratio of retired people to working people in Italy?

(275) Does Italy have a larger manufacturing industry or services industry, as measured by gross revenues?

(276) During ancient Roman times, for what was the Via Salaria used?

(277) The ancient Romans got the idea to use coins as currency from the Greek colonies in Italy. What invention did the ancient Romans make to the coin stamping process that is still used today?

(278) In the mid-19th century, this currency was proclaimed the official currency of Italy by King Emmanuelle II. What is the name for this currency?

(279) Libra was the unit of weight (a pound) ancient Romans employed to set the value of Roman coins. From this Latin word Libra, we derive the word Lira. What abbreviation of Libra is used extensively today to represent weight?

CHAPTER
F·O·U·R
IV

HOLIDAYS, TRADITIONS, & PEOPLE

Uncovering Italian Customs and Civic Life

❝*In a big family the first child is kind of like the first pancake. If it's not perfect, that's okay, there are a lot more coming along.*❞

- ANTONIN SCALIA

❝*When the stars make you drool, just like pasta 'fazool', that's amore.*❞

- "THAT'S AMORE" BY HARRY WARREN

(280) What do Scopa and Briscola have in common?

(281) What group of people were the first to utilize fanfare, including the playing of trumpets and drums, to introduce an announcement of great importance?

(282) How do you say "Happy Easter" in Italian?

(283) Which two Italian cities hosted the 1960 Summer Olympics and the 2006 Winter Olympics?

(284) In what category was Ernesto Moneta awarded the Nobel Prize in 1906?

(285) Born in Chiaraville on August 31, 1870, I am remembered as the first woman to attend medical school in Italy and graduated at age 26 in 1896. I also established a groundbreaking educational system for children. Who am I?

(286) This high-spirited dance, originally popular with the lower classes in Italy, was first performed as a form of courtship and was thought to cure a victim of a tarantula bite by sweating out the poison. Today, this dance is popular with Italian weddings. Name this dance that originated from southern Italy.

(287) Italy leads the rest of Europe in what dubious category as it relates to European immigration?

(288) In Italy, the day after Easter Sunday is often a bigger holiday than Easter itself. This day is referred to as "Little Easter" or Lunedi dell' Angelo. What is the name for this holiday?

(289) In which region of Italy is the German language taught in schools and used in drafting legal documents?

(290) "Pizza di grano", or grain pie, is a favorite food of Italy. During which time of the year is this food traditionally served?

(291) What is Convivio?

(292) Candies and the use of masks, a practice dating to 13th century Venice, are synonymous with Carnevale in Italy. What types of candies are served during Carnevale?

(293) This group of people comprises approximately one of every three (33%) immigrants arriving in Italy today. What is this group?

> ## IT HAPPENED IN...146 B.C.
>
> ▶ **During the Third Punic War, the Roman Army under Scipio Aemilianus defeats the Carthaginians and destroys the city of Carthage. Salt is sprinkled over the land to symbolize its fall and destruction.**

(294) Swiss citizens of German heritage comprise 65% of the Swiss population. What percentage of Swiss citizens of Italian heritage comprise the Swiss population? (a) 2% (b) 10% (c) 25%

(295) Giuseppe Garibaldi, one of the fathers of the Italian unification, became a citizen of this nation in the 1850s and was even offered a commission of major general in this nation's armed forces, which he respectfully declined as he would only serve if given full command of the army. Name this nation.

(296) According to legend, which two brothers, the fabled sons of Mars, the Roman god of war, and Rhea Silvia, the mortal daughter of the king of Alba Longa, are said to have founded Rome?

(297) In America, a person is said to be as "good as gold". Along these same lines, what are people said to be in Italy?

(298) Although only 5% are Italian citizens, many Muslims call Italy home. How many officially registered Muslims are in Italy today?

(299) Which major city in Canada is said to have more Italian neighborhoods than any other city outside of Italy?

(300) Name the ancient tribe of Italy from which Italy/Italia received its name.

(301) This tradition, established around 400 B.C. by the Etruscans and later adopted by the Romans, resulted in the expression "getting a lucky break". This tradition involved hens since they were perceived as having the power of premonition. What is this tradition we have even today?

(302) What Italian national holiday is celebrated on April 25th?

(303) Into which well-known Roman fountain, sculpted by Lorenzo Bernini, can people toss coins to ensure safe returns from their travels? (Hint: featured in the film *Three Coins in the Fountain*)

(304) What are the three largest foreign minority groups in Italy?

(305) The ancient Romans believed that the health and welfare of people changed every seven years. Therefore, what superstition, started and spread by the ancient Romans, could bring seven years of bad luck?

(306) What is the legendary date of the founding for Rome by brothers Remus and Romulus?

(307) Which holiday is celebrated on May 1st in Italy? (Hint: a late summer holiday in America)

(308) Born in Modena on October 12, 1935, I am known as one of the greatest tenors of all time and recognized for my ease at hitting the difficult high C notes with repetition. Who am I?

(309) What do the three colors - green, white and red - of the Italian flag represent?

(310) What is an "edicole sacra"?

(311) Written to remind Italians of their past battles for freedom, this patriotic song was played for the first time on December 1, 1847. Name this song written by Goffredo Mameli and composed by Michele Novaro.

(312) This event, celebrated in Siena on July 2nd and August 16th, pits the city's 17 districts (contrades) against each other in a horserace where horses are selected by lottery and winning for your district is very important. Name this event.

(313) In Italy, school is compulsory until what age?

(314) Now known as the *Mexican Hat Dance*, this dance originated out of southern Italy where the foot was pointed, in contrast to the Mexican version where the foot is flexed. Name the Italian version of this dance.

(315) The Roman symbol of protection was represented by which animal?

(316) What is the origin of the term "Your Valentine"?

TOP 10 OF ITALY
Largest Regions

	REGION	AREA
1	Sicily	25,707
2	Piedmont	25,399
3	Sardinia	24,090
4	Lombardy	23,859
5	Tuscany	22,992
6	Emilia-Romagna	22,125
7	Apulia	19,357
8	Veneto	18,365
9	Lazio	17,227
10	Calabria	15,080

Area is in Square Kilometers
Area Includes Islands

(317) Which tree, commonly found throughout Italy, is symbolic of Italians' love of family, friends, and Mother Nature?

(318) Which two regions in Italy hold the distinctions of the most and the least inhabitants over the age of 100?

(319) What does the annual Maggio Musicale Festival in Florence celebrate?

(320) This celebration includes the traditional Sicilian pasta dishes bucatini con sarde and tubetti con ceci. Pastries such as s'fingi and zeppole are also enjoyed. Name this former national holiday in Italy that is still celebrated today. (Hint: foster father of Jesus)

(321) What is meant by the term "Campanilismo"?

(322) Born in Tuscany on April 15, 1452, I am known as the complete artisan - painter, sculptor, scientist, inventor, writer and engineer. Who am I?

(323) What is the name of the mythical person who brings gifts to Italian children?

(324) Name the popular celebration in Italy where cicerchiata, struffoli, chiacchiere, castagnole and causone are traditional prepared dishes.

(325) For what two reasons is the Colosseum elliptical shaped?

IT HAPPENED IN...324 A.D.

▶**Roman Emperor Constantine establishes the imperial capital in the strategic city of Byzantium, which is renamed Constantinople (present-day Istanbul). In doing so, he reunites the Roman Empire under one authority.**

(326) From which February 15th Roman festival may Saint Valentine's Day have originated?

(327) Approximately how many years did the dynasty of the Medici family of Florence last?

(328) What age group typically attends "Media Superiore", a particular level of education, in Italy?

(329) The Waldinsians is a group of people found predominately in the Piedmont region of Italy. Who are these people?

(330) Which Sicilian festival commemorates the Knights of the Round Table and the Paladins of Charlemagne?

(331) Why does legend hold that Rome was named after Romulus rather than after brother Remus?

(332) Harry Simeone and Henry Onorati are two of the three composers who wrote a 1950 popular Christmas song about a boy and his drum. Name their song.

(333) According to estimates, how many people in Italy will be over the age of 100 by the year 2050?

(334) The vast majority of Italians are Roman Catholic, although there are a small number of Protestants. Approximately how many Protestants live in Italy?

(335) What device for gambling did the ancient Etruscans invent that is used today?

(336) What was the ancient Roman symbol of fertility?

(337) What was the occupation of Mussolini's father?

(338) This traditional charge is levied when you dine at a restaurant in Italy. The charge covers service and bread and is used in lieu of tips. What is the name for this charge?

(339) What is a Ceppo?

(340) These people, known for their spectacular burial chambers in northern and central Italy, typically buried their dead. However, these people were forced to exercise cremation when the Romans conquered and assimilated their civilization. Who are these people?

(341) What did "diploma" refer to during the ancient Roman era?

(342) Born in Pisa on February 15, 1564, I am remembered for inventing the telescope and for my controversial claim that the Sun, and not the Earth, is the center of our galaxy. Who am I?

(343) Passeggiata is a popular and traditional daily event held in many parts of Italy. What is passeggiata?

(344) Which articles of religious clothing has the Italian government banned recently in an attempt to combat terrorism?

(345) Franco Zeffirelli, director of *Tea with Mussolini*, became the first Italian to receive this honor from Queen Elizabeth II of England in 2004 at a lavish ceremony at the British Embassy in Rome. What honor did he receive?

(346) Aside from the imperial family, the Vestal Virgins were the most powerful women in ancient Roman society. What role did these women play?

(347) Why are lovebirds associated with Saint Valentines Day?

TOP 10 OF ITALY
Most Populated Regions

	REGION	POPULATION
1	Lombardy	9,475,202
2	Campania	5,790,929
3	Lazio	5,304,778
4	Sicily	5,017,212
5	Veneto	4,738,313
6	Piedmont	4,341,733
7	Emilia-Romagna	4,187,557
8	Apulia	4,071,518
9	Tuscany	3,619,872
10	Calabria	2,004,415

(348) According to Roman mythology, who was the goddess of love and beauty? (Hint: a famous painting by Botticelli)

(349) During what month of the year is Carnevale typically celebrated?

(350) Contrary to popular belief, the early Christians were not forced to bury their dead in the catacombs underneath Rome because of persecution by the Romans. The early Christians did so for another reason. What was this reason?

(351) During the period 1870 to 1914, which two cities located in the Western Hemisphere had the two largest concentrations of Italian immigrants?

CHAPTER 4

(352) Who are the Bené Roma?

(353) According to Roman mythology, who was the god of the sea?

(354) Approximately 50% of youths between the ages of 18 and 30 still live with their parents in the United Kingdom. In America, this figure is about 40%. What is the approximate percentage for youths still living with their parents in Italy?

(355) During which holiday season will you hear the greeting "Buon Natale"?

(356) This present-day tradition, started by the ancient Romans and said before drinking while raising your glass in a crowd, is used to celebrate a special occasion. This tradition was established as a way for the ancient Romans to absorb the bitterness of wine and make it more healthful. Name this tradition.

(357) Which Brazilian city has the highest concentration of Italians?

(358) What animal was the symbol of liberty in ancient Roman times?

(359) What was the name for the central location in Roman towns and cities where social, political and commerce took place?

(360) How did the Romans celebrate the 1,000 year anniversary of the founding of Rome?

IT HAPPENED IN...476 A.D.

► The ancient Roman Empire collapses. Western emperor, Romulus Augusulus, is deposed by Germanic invaders lead by Odoacer. Only the eastern Roman Empire continues on, but now as the Byzantine Empire.

(361) Born in Genoa in 1451 and died in Spain in 1506, I am remembered for opening the New World to European colonization and for introducing many new and mysterious foods to Europe. Who am I?

(362) Which Italian artist said, "Trifles make perfection and perfection is no trifle"?

(363) What were the five central guidelines by which the ancient Romans lived and governed?

(364) During ancient Roman times, what was given to a gladiator to signify his freedom, usually the result of winning many victories and becoming a favorite of the fans?

(365) The book, *Dialogue on the Great World Systems*, got which Renaissance author and scientist in hot water with the Vatican?

(366) According to Roman mythology, this god was the son of Venus and Mercury. Name this god (similar to the Greek god Eros) known for his match making and arrow shooting.

(367) What stray animal does the city of Rome have more of, per square mile, than any other city in the world?

(368) Born in Florence on November 3, 1500, I was called "the greatest goldsmith of whom the world has ever heard" by Michelangelo. However, I am most remembered for writing what is considered by many to be the most famous autobiography in the world. Who am I?

(369) What was the Bachelor Tax?

(370) Where in Italy are the two largest and most popular Carnevale festivals held?

(371) The idea of hosting gladiatorial fights originated from what gruesome practice?

(372) According to Roman mythology, which god is the supreme deity? (Hint: Italian sky god and the largest planet in our solar system)

(373) Born in Florence on May 3, 1469, I am known for my politically cunning book, *The Prince*. Who am I?

(374) On which day of the year can you hear the greeting "Felice Capo d'Anno" in Italy?

> # IT HAPPENED IN...241 B.C.
>
> ▶**The Roman Navy defeats the Carthaginian fleet at the battle of the Aegates (Egadi) Islands. As a result of their defeat, Carthage surrenders Sicily to the Romans and sues for peace.**

(375) This type of card game in Italy dates at least back 400 years and probably longer. This card game, meaning "sweep, broom", has two versions - a classic version and three-card version. Name this card game.

(376) According to Roman mythology, who is the goddess of fortune and chance?

(377) What was different about Leonardo da Vinci's diet?

(378) Now a popular tourist attraction, this modern-day British city was once home to elaborate Roman baths built around the many natural hot springs located throughout the area. Name this city.

(379) According to a recent poll, which country do the majority of Italians view as the best alternative to living in Italy?

(380) What percentage of Italians considers themselves Roman Catholic?

(381) Italian Ciriaco de Pizzicolli (or D'Ancona Ciriaco), a 15th century scholar, is considered the first person of record to uncover and investigate past civilizations. What profession did he thus introduce?

(382) These small particles of suspended copper give Murano beads their sparkle in light. What is the name for these small particles?

(383) At traditional Italian weddings, confetti (almond candies) are placed in decorative bags called bomboniere and given with each wedding favor. What do each of the five confetti symbolize?

(384) What is the standard Italian telephone greeting?

(385) For what reason can you find fair-skinned, blue-eyed, and blond Sicilians?

(386) Where in Italy is the "Festival of the Two Worlds" held?

(387) How many official holidays in Italy are based on Roman Catholic holy days?

CHAPTER F·I·V·E

HOLY CATHOLIC CHURCH & THE VATICAN

Little Known Facts and Figures

"While you are proclaiming peace with your lips, be careful to have it even more fully in your heart."

- SAINT FRANCIS OF ASSISI

"The first idea the child must acquire is that of the difference between good and evil."

- MARIA MONTESSORI

(388) In the Vatican, the pope's high alter stands over the grave of which combination disciple/pope/saint?

(389) What religious order is traditionally in charge of Vatican Radio?

(390) Giovanni Pierluigi da Palestrina is considered the first musician of what organization?

(391) Which play, made into a television show starring Burt Lancaster, was written by John Paul II in 1960?

(392) During World War II, Pope Pius XI and Pope Pius XII would leave the Vatican for their summer residence to avoid a certain world leader. The popes even closed the Sistine Chapel for "repairs" to keep this leader from seeing the inside, a goal of his. Name this world leader not well-liked by the popes.

(393) What restriction does the Vatican have on their airspace?

(394) Is the election of pope conducted by secret or open ballot?

(395) The catacombs of Rome were used extensively for what purpose during the late ancient Roman era?

(396) The father of Padre Pio lived in New York City for a time. What was the occupation of the elder Pio?

(397) This annual tax was originally levied on English house owners in the early 10th century to financially support the Catholic Church. Name this now voluntary donation collected throughout the Church.

(398) What is a "Papal Bull"?

(399) Only one Catholic order can absolve the sins of the pope. Name this Catholic order.

(400) Who is the patron saint of Italy and when is his feast day celebrated?

(401) What does canon law require be enclosed in every Catholic church and chapel?

(402) What do the following share in common - Carmine, Apostoli, Orsanmichele and Santo Spirito?

(403) In the early 14th century, the papacy was moved temporarily from Rome to which European city?

(404) What is a stigmata?

(405) After each voting session for a new pope, what is done with the ballots?

(406) What type of vegetation, commonly found in Italy, did Noah first see after the water began to recede?

(407) The life of which saint is depicted on the doors of the Baptistery of Florence?

(408) Buried at the Vatican is a famous 17th century European Queen. Name her.

(409) Born in Assisi in 1181, I founded the Franciscan Order in 1209. Who am I?

(410) Who is the Madonna?

(411) Who said to Pope Julius II, "Your Blessedness, when it is finished!"?

(412) What did Pope Gregory XIII do in 1582 to bring the then calendar in line with the natural pattern of the seasons?

(413) Which church was the first in Italy dedicated to the Virgin Mary?

(414) Simon Bar-Jona is the birth name of which saint?

(415) What is a "nuncio"?

(416) What is the name for the free-standing bell towers in Italian churches?

(417) Who founded the Franciscan Order of nuns?

(418) What is the largest Catholic University in Europe?

(419) The four letters, I N R I, were inscribed at the top of the cross used to crucify Christ. What words do these four letters represent?

(420) This cloth was used to wrap Christ's body for burial. Today, this cloth is housed in the Duomo di San Giovanni in Turin, Italy. What is the name of this cloth?

(421) Umbria is the birthplace of many saints. Which saint, today known for match making, was born in Umbria?

(422) Jesus means Joshua in Hebrew and Yeshua in Aramaic. However, all three names mean the same thing. What do they all mean?

(423) What plan did Pope Pius XII have in the event of arrest by Adolf Hitler?

(424) This town hosted the Council of Trent, an eighteen year event that gave birth to the Counter Reformation movement. Name this town.

(425) What is the affectionate name given to the patron saint of Italy, Saint Francis of Assisi, who was committed to a life of poverty?

(426) In which year did Vatican Radio first air and who was the first person to broadcast?

(427) Vatican City, the smallest state in the world, is approximately 0.2 square miles and records about 700 citizens. What defines the border between Vatican City and Italy, specifically Rome?

(428) This saint was crucified under Roman Emperor Nero in A.D. 60. Per his request, he was crucified upside down on the cross because he did not believe that he deserved to be crucified in the same manner as Christ. Name this early saint.

(429) What is the name of the official Vatican newspaper?

> **IT HAPPENED IN...410 A.D.**
>
> ►Rome is attacked and overrun by the Visigoths under the command of Alaric. Resistance to stop the "barbarians" is weak.

(430) What did Pope John Paul II carry around with him when traveling?

(431) Who is the patron saint of Florence?

(432) Saint Mark is the patron saint of Venice, although this was not always the case. Prior to the consecration of the Basilica of Saint Mark, which saint was the patron saint of Venice?

(433) Although Christianity was granted freedom of worship by Emperor Constantine, which emperor made Christianity the official religion of the Roman Empire in 380 A.D.?

(434) When electing a new pope, how many times each day are ballots cast by the College of Cardinals?

(435) What distinction does the Tuscan Countess Matilda Canossa hold?

(436) What is the significance of the Edict of Milan in 313 A.D.?

(437) The Treaty of Lateran Pacts, signed by both Italy and the Catholic Church in 1929, established what state?

(438) Who is the patron saint of Sicily?

(439) Established in 1505 by Pope Julius II, this group is charged with protecting the pope. The first group consisted of 150 mercenaries who marched to the pope's aid. Name this group.

(440) Why do Catholic cardinals typically wear vestments in the color red?

(441) The ancient Romans were known for their tolerance of different religions and allowed freedom of worship. Why then did the Romans persecute the early Christians?

(442) Did Pope John Paul II ever receive a large inheritance?

(443) Born in Bologna in 1774, Father Giuseppe Gaspare Mezzofanti, called the greatest linguist of all time, was known for his fluency in many languages. In how many languages was he fluent?

(444) When Polish Cardinal Karol Wojtyla became Pope John Paul II in 1978, he became the first non-Italian pope in how many years? (a) 77 (b) 123 (c) 456

(445) What is the name of the summer residence in Italy used by popes since the 17th century?

(446) Who is the patron saint of Rome?

(447) Which leading American city is named after Saint Francis of Assisi?

(448) Where in Vatican City does the pope live?

(449) What is the traditional weapon of the Swiss Guard, the personal bodyguards of the pope?

CHAPTER 5

(450) Which Italian saint is honored by Scandinavians, especially in Sweden?

(451) Name the dictator who supposedly said, "So, tell me, how many (military) divisions does the pope have?".

(452) Which six languages did Pope John Paul II speak?

(453) This veil is said to have the imprinted image of Christ's face. The image was received after the veil was used to wipe Christ's face while he carried the cross at his crucifixion. Name this famous veil.

(454) Born in Aquino in 1225, I am known as "The Prince of Theologians" for my Catholic teachings based on logic and reason rather than faith and revelation. I am also known for my vow of poverty as a member of the Dominican Order. Who am I?

(455) What is said to happen when the blood of Saint Gennaro, the patron saint of Naples, liquefies when it is brought out once per year?

(456) What was the Franciscan Order originally named by its founder Saint Francis of Assisi?

(457) Which group is responsible for assisting in the decision making and in running of the Papacy?

(458) What title is sometimes bestowed on priests as a mark of papal recognition?

TOP 10 OF ITALY

Most Densely Populated Regions

	REGION	POPULATION
1	Campania	426
2	Lombardy	397
3	Lazio	308
4	Liguria	297
5	Veneto	249
6	Apulia	208
7	Sicily	195
8	Emila-Romagna	189
9	Piedmont	167
10	Tuscany	158

People per Square Kilometer

(459) Which religious order is otherwise known as Society of Jesus?

(460) Which Italian saint started the Christmas custom of restaging the Nativity scene to commemorate the birth of Jesus?

(461) Where in Italy can you find a painting of the crucifixion that is said to have spoken to Saint Thomas Aquinas?

(462) Which well known Italian saint wrote *Cantico delle Creature*?

(463) What is the income tax rate for citizens of Vatican City?

(464) This language was spoken by Jesus and his disciples. Today, this language is relatively forgotten as it was replaced by the Arabic language. What is this language, the language Christ and his disciples spoke?

(465) Has there ever been a pope of Jewish heritage?

(466) This Italian saint was born Giovanni Bernardone, a name later changed to Francis Francisco by his father. Name this saint.

IT HAPPENED IN...527 A.D.

▶Justinian becomes the emperor of the eastern Roman Empire. His Digest or Pandects become the foundation of European legal code for centuries.

(467) During the period of 1522 to 1978, a total of 456 consecutive years, every pope was of which ethnic heritage?

(468) When did Michelangelo begin and end his work on the Sistine Chapel?

(469) Which comedian was arrested at the Vatican for impersonating a priest?

(470) This position within the Vatican requires men to be Swiss citizens, be at least six feet tall, and be between the ages of 18 and 25. In addition, these men must sign an agreement to serve a two year term. Name this position.

(471) To signal that a new pope was not elected, black smoke is released from the Vatican. What is added to the ballots and burnt to produce this black smoke?

(472) Italian legend holds that the donkey that Christ rode on into Jerusalem was given a symbol on its back and shoulders as a reward for its service. What symbol did the donkey receive?

(473) By the end of the 4th century A.D., all citizens of the Roman Empire were required to practice which faith?

(474) What form of the Latin language, sometimes referred to as "church Latin", is the standard language for official documents of the Catholic Church?

(475) What strange benefit did Pope Paul III give to Michelangelo for his contributions to the Catholic Church?

(476) The Jesuit Order established its very first school for boys in 1548. In which Italian city was this school established?

(477) Who was the first pope from Poland?

(478) Born in Rome in 1545, Giulio Cassini is known for writing this classic Catholic song honoring the Blessed Virgin Mary. Name this song.

(479) In A.D. 325, Roman Emperor Constantine convened a council and made two decrees related to early Christianity. What were these landmark decrees? (Hint: one established an important date and one established an important symbol)

(480) What is the basic origin of Carnevale?

(481) In which year was Padre Pio beautified by Pope John Paul II?

(482) Pope John Paul II gave one of the bullets that struck him in the 1981 assassination attempt to the Shrine of Our Lady of Fatima church. In which country is this church located?

(483) Where was Pope John Paul II nearly assassinated by gunfire in 1981 from Turkish Bulgarian Mehmet Ali Agca?

(484) Pope Pius VI established the first Catholic diocese in the United States on April 6, 1789. Name the American city where this diocese was established.

(485) What is the name for the skullcap worn by bishops and other prelates?

(486) What pagan tradition in ancient Rome led to gift giving by Christians at Christmas time?

(487) The second largest religious procession in the world is held in Catania, Sicily on February 5th. Which feast day do Sicilians celebrate on this day?

(488) This saint founded the Abbey of Monte Cassino and established the "Rule of Saint Benedict" in 530 A.D. that founded the Benedictine Order of monks. Name this saint.

(489) Who is the patron saint of Milan?

(490) What wild animal did Saint Francis of Assisi tame?

(491) The modern Saint Peter's Basilica was built atop an older basilica erected by Constantine. In what year was the new Saint Peter's Basilica consecrated? (a) 1056 (b) 1401 (c) 1626

(492) During the early days of the Christian Church when persecution was widespread and frequent, what food did Christians serve as a secret code to identify other Christians?

(493) What is the birth name of Pope John Paul II?

(494) What minimal salary do popes receive from the Vatican for their service?

(495) Saint Benedict, the founder of the Benedictine Order, and his twin sister are buried together at the Abbey of Monte Cassino. Name this twin sister and saint.

(496) This person is considered the second most important person at the Vatican after the pope himself. This person performs many tasks similar to those of senior level diplomats. What is the title of this person?

(497) According to the Vatican, how often should bishops meet with the pope?

(498) This structure encompasses 430,000 square feet and can accommodate 20,000 people in its expansive area. Name this structure that is the largest church and Cathedral in all of Christendom.

(499) In response to a deadly plague enveloping Italy during the 6th century A.D., Pope Gregory I replaced the expression "Good luck to you", often said when someone sneezed (a sneeze was thought to be a precursor to a deadly illness), with what now common expression?

(500) Born on May 25, 1887 in the town of Pietreclina in the province of Benevento, I am known for having received the stigmata on numerous occasions. The first such event occurred on September 20, 1918. Who am I?

(501) He was born Fernando de Bouillon in Portugal during the 12th century and is one of most popular saints in Italy. Who is he?

(502) The great Bishop of Milan, known for having converted Augustine (later to become Saint Augustine), introduced church hymn singing in A.D. 386. Name this saint.

(503) This saint was the first recorded person to receive the stigmata (the marks of the crucifixion of Jesus Christ) in 1224 after 40 days of fasting. He received the stigmata frequently during the last two years of his life before dying in 1226. Name this saint.

(504) What are the seven rites of Catholicism?

(505) Which pope scheduled his introductory ceremony as new pope around a soccer match?

(506) What is the longest amount of time in history the cardinals needed to elect a new pope?

(507) This fresco, produced by Michelangelo in 1541, is the largest fresco produced during the Renaissance. Name this fresco.

(508) How did Pope John Paul II nearly lose his life during his childhood?

(509) What pivotal event happened to Saint Peter while traveling the Via Appia?

(510) This theologian is credited with writing over fifty works that logically and objectively defending the Catholic Church and its doctrines. His most famous work and masterpiece, *Summa Theologica*, is an exposition of theology and a summary of Christian philosophy. Name this saint.

(511) What is the primary responsibility of the Curia Romana?

(512) Who was the Roman procurator (governor) of Judea in the early 1st century A.D. that questioned and crucified Jesus?

(513) What is *L'Osservatore Romano*?

(514) What is the official language of the Catholic Church?

CHAPTER
S·I·X
VI

GOVERNMENT, ORGANIZATION, & LEADERSHIP

Trailblazing Italian Statesmen and Their Contributions

"Benefits should be conferred gradually; and in that way they will taste better."

- NICCOLO MACHIAVELLI

"I affirm that the doctrine of Machiavelli is more alive today than it was four centuries ago."

- BENITO MUSSOLINI

55

(515) This holiday celebrates the official birth of the Italian Republic on June 2, 1946. Name this holiday.

(516) What unwanted honor of distinction does 5th century Roman Emperor Augustus Romulus hold?

(517) In which city did Mussolini begin the Fascist movement?

IT HAPPENED IN...572 A.D.

▶**The Longobards, a Germanic tribe from the Danube river area, invades Italy, captures Pavia and establishes their capital. The area to the north and east becomes Longobardia and later Lombardia.**

(518) What is the official state religion of Italy?

(519) Written by Goffredo Mameli, *Fratelli d' Italia* is better known as which song?

(520) How long after the disintegration of the ancient Roman Empire did it take to bring Italy under unified control without foreign interference?

(521) In 27 B.C. the Roman Republic morphed into the Roman Empire. Name the person considered the first truly appointed emperor of Rome.

(522) In what year was the current Italian constitution drafted?

(523) Which Italian city was proclaimed the first capital of the Kingdom of Italy upon unification in 1861?

(524) Approximately how many residents did the ancient Roman Empire have at its peak?

(525) This person was the last king of Italy. His reign lasted for 26 days before a referendum ended the monarchy shortly after World War II. Name him.

(526) The writings of which Roman statesman greatly influenced and helped develop the concept of a society based on liberty?

(527) Which group of people during the middle part of the 20th century does the word "fuorusciti" describe?

(528) How tall was Benito Mussolini? (a) 5'7" (b) 5'9" (c) 6'3"

(529) Mussolini gave himself the nickname "Il Duce". What does this mean in English?

TOP 10 OF ITALY
Highest Birthrates by Region

	REGION	RATE
1	Campania	12.4
2	Bolzano	12.3
3	Sicily	11.3
4	Trentino-Alto Adige	11.3
5	Apulia	10.9
6	Calabria	10.4
7	Trento	10.3
8	Basilicata	10.0
9	Veneto	9.2
10	Lazio	9.0

Birthrate per 1000 People

(530) How many kings ruled ancient Rome before the formation of the Roman Republic in 509 B.C. when Etruscan King Tarquin was deposed?

(531) Under the current Italian system of government, who is the only person who can dissolve parliament and call for new elections?

(532) This Italian became the ruler of Kingdom of Piedmont-Sardinia in 1852 and secretly devised a plan to instigate a war between Austria-Hungary and Kingdom of Piedmont-Sardinia, with French assistance. This war led to the unification of Italy. Name this man.

(533) Before Rome became the capital of Italy after unification in the 19th century, which other two cities held that same distinction for a brief time?

(534) In which Italian city were the secret meetings of the Carbonari, the group that sparked Italian unification, held and led by Giuseppe Mazzini?

(535) On what date was Mussolini named prime minister of Italy?

(536) Under which Roman general's rise to absolute power signaled the end of the ancient Roman Republic, thus planting the seeds of the Roman Empire?

(537) Benito Mussolini established the Fascist party in the early 20th century. For what was the original purpose of this organization?

(538) In 1946, Italians went to the polls to vote on a referendum to become a republic or to stay a monarchy. The vote was surprisingly close, although the result did favor becoming a republic. What percentage of Italian voters barely elected to change to a republic and oust the monarchy?

(539) Charlton Heston played the great Renaissance artist and sculptor, Michelangelo, in what Hollywood movie?

(540) Who is considered the greatest of all the Medici, a family that ruled Florence during the Renaissance?

(541) The Medici family of Florence selected 3rd century saints Cosmas and Damian as their patron saints. For what reason were these two specifically selected?

(542) How many judges comprise the Constitutional Court, the supreme arbiter of Italian justice?

(543) This governmental institution serves as the basic administration unit for both regions and provinces. This institution, sometimes referred to as the Municipio, provides many basic civil functions and is housed in a building commonly called the Palazzo Comunale. Name this institution.

(544) The Carbonari was a group formed during the 18th century in Italy. This group was named for hot black coal because of their passion to a specific cause. Who were the Carbonari?

(545) Mussolini and the Fascists were opposed to which two political systems prevalent in Europe at the time?

(546) What accomplishments is Mussolini known for?

(547) English and American "Common Law" is rooted in and takes much of its basis of law from what legal system?

(548) The English word "justice", as it relates to the legal system, is named for which Roman emperor who implemented and fostered advances in the Roman legal system?

> ### IT HAPPENED IN...827 A.D.
>
> ▶The Saracens, or Muslims, invade the island of Sicily and seize the entire island when the last Byzantine stronghold of Taormina falls. The city of Bari on the peninsula is captured soon thereafter and ruled by Moroccan emirs for 30 years.

(549) This person introduced the term "Axis" to describe the German and Italian alliance in World War II. He used the term to reference how all other European nations would revolve around Germany and Italy. Name this person who coined "Axis" powers.

(550) Born in Predappio on July 29, 1893, I was a school teacher and journalist turned Italian dictator. My nickname was "Il Doce". Who am I?

(551) Under the current Italian system of government, who are the only people able to dismiss a prime minister using a no-confidence vote?

(552) This American World War II general, a history buff, took great pride in marching his troops over ancient Roman roads and bridges in honor of the great generals of the Roman era who did the same. Name this general.

(553) Under Mussolini, having numerous children was considered patriotic. Therefore, what did Italian families receive when they had five or more children?

(554) What aspect of the U.S. electoral system is based on the ancient Roman Republic form of election?

(555) What distinction does Pietro Badoglio, a 20th century Italian politician, hold?

(556) How many linguistic minorities are recognized by the Italian constitution and laws?

(557) The mysterious Etruscans are thought to have immigrated from Eastern Europe or perhaps from Asia Minor. Approximately when did Etruscan society begin in Italy and how long did it last?

(558) "Black Shirts" was the name given to the Fascist followers of this leader that forcefully seized power in Italy on October 28, 1922 with their legendary "March on Rome". Name this leader.

(559) This Italian organized a political society called "La Giovine Italia" or "Young Italy". His motto was "Dio e il Popolo" or "God and the people". Name this great leader of the Italian reunification.

(560) Which Italian city was the first to fly the modern Italian flag in the 19th century?

(561) Born in Nice on July 4, 1807, I am known as one of the fathers of Italian unification with the Italian National Anthem named in honor of me. Who am I?

(562) What symbols were present on the Italian flag, but removed when Italy became a Republic in 1946?

(563) In 1957, Italy became one of the six founding members of the European Union. In which Italian city was this historic organization established by treaty?

(564) How many popes and queens did the powerful Medici family of Florence provide?

(565) Although Napoleon was born in Corsica, an island sold by the Italian city-state of Genoa to France in 1768, his family was not French. His family emigrated from Italy to Corsica in the 18th century. From which region did his family leave?

(566) What was the Salo Republic?

(567) On which of the "Seven Hills of Rome" were built the ancient Roman royal palaces?

(568) What was the name of Mussolini's yacht?

(569) In what year was abortion legalized in Italy?

(570) What agenda does the Lega Nord (Northern League) promote?

(571) Which Roman general said the famous expression "The die is cast" on his march across the Rubicon into Italy?

(572) Mussolini wanted to make what change to the calendar?

(573) What was the Pact of Steel treaty of 1939?

(574) The leading family of Florence during the Renaissance was the Medici. What family was the counterpart of the Medici in Milan during the Renaissance?

(575) In what year did women win the right to vote in Italy?

(576) On what day was the Kingdom of Italy proclaimed by parliament, thus unifying Italy?

(577) This emperor split the Roman Empire into two smaller empires - a Western Roman Empire under the control of Rome and an eastern Roman Empire under the control of Byzantium (later renamed Constantinople). Name this emperor.

(578) This man was one of the fathers of the Roman Republic and one of the first two consuls of Rome. He is also an ancestor to the friend, turned assassin, who stabbed Julius Caesar to death many years later. Name this person.

IT HAPPENED IN...1094 A.D.

▶The Basilica of Saint Mark is consecrated in Venice. Entombed in the basilica is the body of Saint Mark. His body, kept in Alexandria since the 1st century, was smuggled out along with pieces of pork to bypass Muslim custom inspectors.

(579) How many popes and queens did the powerful Medici family of Florence provide?

(580) After Mussolini and his mistress were captured and shot to death, what was done with their corpses?

(581) Although seldom initiated by Italian couples, what was made legal in the early 1970s? (Hint: prevalent in America)

(582) This major Italian city did not originally join the Kingdom of Italy when Italy was unified in 1861. However, this city did join in 1871 when occupying French forces left the city and Italian forces subsequently liberated the city from foreign rule. Name this city.

(583) This man, a native of Thrace, served as a legionnaire in the Roman army before deserting and, after his capture, became a slave and eventually a legendary gladiator. In 73 A.D., he escaped from the town of Capua and led a revolt of Roman slaves and gladiators that terrorized southern Italy. Name this mighty figure in Roman history.

(584) In which year was the Communist Party of Italy first established?

(585) Although the Kingdom of Italy was established in 1861, Rome did not join immediately due to French occupation of the city. In which year was Rome liberated and proclaimed the capital of the Kingdom of Italy?

(586) Giuseppe Garibaldi, Giuseppe Mazzini and Camille Benso Cavour were highly influential in which great Italian struggle of the 19th century?

(587) The eastern Roman Empire lasted until 1453 A.D., nearly a 1,000 years after the fall of Rome, until its collapse at the hands of the Muslim Turks under Sultan Mehmet II. By which other name do we know the eastern Roman Empire?

(588) This political movement culminated in the unification of Italy in 1861. What was the name for this movement?

(589) In 1948, a constitutional amendment was past restricting who from ever stepping foot in Italy?

(590) What do 18-5642TC, 11-4201TC and 18-1661TC have in common?

(591) In 166 A.D., Roman Emperor Marcus Aurelius sent an embassy to what far off civilization?

(592) Born in Genoa on June 22, 1805, I am known for my work in unifying Italy in the 1800s and am often referred to as the "father of the Italian nation". Who am I?

(593) Giuseppe Garibaldi is regarded as the George Washington of Italy. What was the nickname of Giuseppe Garibaldi's volunteer fighting force during the struggle for Italian unification?

(594) What is the highest award that Italy bestows on a non-resident?

(595) This Roman emperor presided over the completion of the Roman Colosseum, destroyed Jerusalem in 70 A.D., and built the famous arch still standing in Rome. Who is he?

(596) In which year was the occupying French garrison in Rome forced to withdraw because of the Franco-Prussian War and the city subsequently seized by Italian forces, thus leading to unification with the Kingdom of Italy?

(597) What are the names of the two Italian houses of parliament?

CHAPTER
S·E·V·E·N
VII

ITALIAN AMERICANS & IMMIGRATION

Italian Heritage and People Outside of Italy

"I would like to be known not for the heights I have reached, but for the depths from which I have risen."

- CONNIE FRANCIS

"Every American was once an immigrant."

- FIERELLO LA GUARDIA

65

(598) What honor of distinction does the Fratellanza Society, founded in Saint Louis in 1866, hold?

(599) This Italian American actor starred in such movies as *Home Alone*, *Lethal Weapon*, *Goodfellas*, and *Raging Bull*, the movie which earned him an Oscar nomination for Best Supporting Actor. Name this actor.

(600) This Italian American is the only jockey to ride two Triple Crown winners during a career spanning victories in five Derbies, six Preaknesses and six Belmonts. Name this jockey who began his career in 1931.

(601) Born near Rome on January 6, 1895, I am known as the legendary "Scarface". Who am I?

(602) What is the birth name of singer and entertainer Johnny Desmond?

(603) At the beginning of the 20th century, approximately what percentage of workers of the New York City Department of Public Works were Italian American or Italian?

(604) What is the birth name of Italian American rock star Jon Bon Jovi, born in 1962 in New Jersey?

(605) Born Nicolas Coppola in 1964, this Italian American actor is the nephew of Francis Ford Coppola, the prominent film producer. Nicolas changed his name because he wanted to be judged on his own talents and merits. Name this actor.

(606) Approximately what percentage of the United States armed forces during World War I was Italian American?

(607) This person became one of the first American citizens of Italian heritage. He was also a spy and financier for the American cause during the American War of Independence and even aided George Rogers Clark on his exploration of the Northwest Territory in the late 18th century. Name him.

(608) Which city in the United States boasts the most Italian Americans?

(609) What two-week long summer feast is celebrated in New York City honoring the patron saint of Naples?

(610) What did Italian American Vincent Ciccono, inventor of the "blow pop", invent to combat the effects of the common cold?

(611) Which 19th century American president was awarded an honorary citizenship from the Republic of San Marino?

> ## IT HAPPENED IN...1204 A.D.
>
> ▶ **Pope Innocent III calls for the Fourth Crusade. The Venetians, under contract to ship the Crusaders to Palestine, instead convince the Crusaders to plunder Constantinople on their way to the Holy Land. Venice gains wealth and expands its empire.**

(612) In the United States, are there more cities named after Florence, Venice or Genoa?

(613) Gaetano Lanza, born in 1848 in the United States to Sicilian immigrants, developed the first wind tunnel in 1909 and founded the engineering department at arguably the most prestigious technological university in the world. Name this university, the place where Lanza taught for 36 years.

(614) What two distinct military honors were bestowed on John Basilone, a U.S. Marine gunnery sergeant and Italian American from Buffalo, New York, for his bravery at the battles of Guadalcanal and Iwo Jima during World War II?

(615) This brand of coffeemaker, invented by Italian American Vince Marotta from Cleveland, is the best selling coffeemaker in the world. Name the brand of coffeemaker.

(616) This Italian American actor starred in the television series Taxi and in such movies as *Twins*, *L.A. Confidential* and *One Flew Over the Cuckoo's Nest*. Name him.

(617) What famous singer and entertainer changed his name from Dino Crocetti?

(618) This intense Oakland Raider's defensive lineman was named the NFL's Defensive Player of the Year in 1977. Name this fifteen year NFL veteran.

(619) Born in Hoboken, New Jersey on December 12, 1915, I am known as "Chairman of the Board". I earned an Academy Award for acting and transformed American pop music with songs such as *My Way* and *New York, New York*. Who am I?

(620) Joe DiMaggio married this very popular actress on January 15, 1954 at San Francisco's City Hall. After her death, he ensured that flowers were delivered to her crypt every week for over twenty years. Name this actress.

(621) American President Thomas Jefferson built his private estate in Virginia using architectural contributions from Italian Andrea Palladio. Furthermore, the Italian name Jefferson gave his estate translates to "little mountain". What was the name of his estate?

(622) What father and son combination accepted four Academy Awards for the movie, *Godfather, Part II*?

(623) Which state did politician Peter Domenici represent in the U.S. Congress?

(624) On which type of American currency, circulated during the early half of the 20th century, could you find the image of Italian American Maria Teresa Cafarelli?

(625) In which world heritage category does UNESCO rank Italy number one?

(626) What was the original name for the Radio Corporation of America, or RCA? (Hint: inventor of the radio)

(627) This great Italian American boxer was born Rocco Francis Marchegiano in 1923 in Brockton, Massachusetts. By which name do we know him better?

(628) This food celebrity, the daughter of an Italian American mother, has four Food Network shows. In addition, she is a well-known author for her 30 minute meals books and was married in Italy in 2006. Name her.

(629) Born on May 1, 1967, I am the son of a famous relief pitcher for New York and Philadelphia and the son of an Italian American mother. I attended Northeast Louisiana University on a baseball scholarship and dropped out to pursue a career in music. Today, I am one of the most successful country music stars and married to famous country music star Faith Hill. Who am I?

(630) This Italian American actor starred in *Goodfellas* and had a supporting role in *Field of Dreams*. Name him.

(631) What Baltimore Oriole's baseball player shares the record for the most grand slams in a single season, a feat accomplished in 1961?

(632) The late great artist, Liberace, was Italian on his father's side. What heritage was he on his mother's side?

(633) U.S. Army Air Force Captain Don Gentile, born in Ohio to Italian immigrant parents, was awarded the Distinguished Service Cross during World War II, and personally pinned by Supreme Allied Commander Dwight D. Eisenhower. For what reason was this done?

(634) What story did Al Capone originally tell people about how he obtained his two three-inch scars, actually received from a knife fight, on his left cheek?

(635) What do Nancy Barbato, Ava Gardner, Mia Farrow and Barbara Marx have in common?

(636) Which U.S. state became the first state to observe Columbus Day in 1905?

(637) What black Italian American was a football legend with the Pittsburgh Steelers?

(638) Approximately 65% of the first Italian immigrants to Milwaukee, Wisconsin came from one particular region in Italy. Name this region.

(639) Yogi Berra was born Lawrence Peter Berra on May 12, 1925. In which city was he born?

(640) Approximately what percentage of Italian immigrants used Ellis Island as their point of entry to America?

(641) Anthony Conza and Fred De Luca each founded leading global sandwich companies. Name the two companies these Italian Americans founded.

(642) Which Italian American was elected chairman and CEO of the New York Stock Exchange in 1985, but forced out in the mid-2000s?

(643) In 1999, Catherine De Angelis became the first women editor for which prestigious medical journal published in the United States?

(644) This Italian American, born Harry Christopher Carabina, was the longtime voice of the Chicago Cubs from 1945 until his death in 1997. Name this fan favorite radio announcer who was known for his renditions of *Take Me Out to the Ballgame* at Wrigley Field.

CHAPTER 7

(645) Established in 1849 by businessman Secchi de Casale in New York City, this newspaper was the first Italian-language newspaper published in the United States. Name this publication.

(646) Born on December 19, 1972, I am known for my versatile acting for both television and the movie screen. I gained fame on the television program *Who's the Boss* and presently star in the television series *Charmed*. Who am I?

(647) Born in Flushing, New York on November 17, 1942, I left the seminary to attend New York University's film school where I received bachelors and masters degrees. I am known for my brilliant directing, including the box office hits *The Color of Money*, *Goodfellas* and *Cassino*. Who am I?

(648) This Italian American actor starred in *Bull Durham* and *Thelma and Louise*. In 1996, she won the Academy Award for Best Actress for *Dead Man Walking*. Name her.

(649) This Italian American organization was founded by successful businessman Jeno Paulucci. One of their goals is "to preserve and protect Italian American heritage and culture and to encourage the teaching of Italian language and culture in U.S. schools". Name this Washington, D.C. based organization.

(650) This person won the American League Manager of the Year award four times (1974, 1976, 1980, and 1981) and in 1977 became the first Italian American manager to win a World Series. Name this former Yankees manager.

(651) An Italian American was the first Catholic priest to be appointed Chaplain of the United States Senate in 1832. Name this priest.

(652) President John F. Kennedy appointed the first Italian American to be Secretary of Health, Education and Welfare. Name this appointee.

(653) Eddie Arcano competed in over 24,000 events, winning nearly 25% of those events and earning over $30 million in the process. Name this sport. (a) golf (b) grand prix racing (c) horse racing

(654) This large money-center bank, formally named the Bank of Italy, was established by Amadeo Pietro Giannini, the son of Genoese immigrants. This bank was the largest commercial bank in the world during the 1930s. Name this present-day bank.

(655) Disney's EPCOT center in Orlando, Florida uses an Italian city as the setting for one of its attractions. Name this Italian city.

(656) The Royal Italian, Third Piemonte and 13th Du Perche were the names of three military regiments from Italy. In which American war did they fight?

(657) This Italian American actor got his start on the television series *Taxi*, and followed it up with *Who's the Boss*. Name this actor.

(658) Al Caiola, a musical arranger, wrote the theme song for what 1950s television series? (a) *The Lone Ranger* (b) *Bonanza* (c) *Dragnet*

(659) Born Lewis Pessano in Tyaskin, Maryland in 1858, Buttercup Dickerson was a professional baseball player in the 19th century. He began his seven year career as an outfielder with Cincinnati. What honor of distinction does he hold?

IT HAPPENED IN...1288 A.D.

▶ **Genoa and Pisa conclude their war and make peace. Pisa is forced to cede the islands of Elba and Corsica to Genoa, however, Genoa destroys Pisa's harbor when they refuse to cede the territories. The destruction of the harbor forever prohibits Pisa from once again becoming a maritime power.**

(660) This newspaper, established more than four decades ago, is the leading Italian American newspaper in Chicago and one of the top in America. Name this newspaper based in Stone Park, Illinois and published by Anthony J. Fornelli.

(661) The town of Pio Nomo in the state of Georgia is named in honor of which Catholic pope?

(662) This Italian American actor, the son of an Italian immigrant mother from Calabria, starred in such movies as *Under Siege* and *Fire Down Below*. Name this action packed actor known for his martial arts fighting.

(663) This New Orleans band, formed in 1914 by Dominick "Nick" La Rocca and Anthony Sbarbaro, is credited with inventing a certain type of jazz music, which is named after their band. Their famous song, *Tiger Rag* - now known as *Hold that Tiger* - is the official song of the Louisiana State University. Name this band.

(664) This great University of Notre Dame quarterback won the national college football championship in 1977 and played for the San Francisco 49ers in route to winning four SuperBowls. He passed for 40,551 yards and 273 touchdowns in his highly accomplished career. Name him.

(665) This Italian American attended Saint Marymount in New York City and was the first woman nominated for vice-president of the United States. Name her.

(666) Born Anna Maria Louise Italiano in 1932 in New York, this actor won the Best Actress Oscar in 1962 for her performance in *The Miracle Worker* and won the Golden Globe award in 1968 for her role in the *The Graduate*. Name this actor.

(667) Bancroft Gerardi was the first Italian American to attain what U.S. military rank in the mid-1800s? (a) Field Marshall (b) Cavalry Captain (c) Admiral

(668) In 1954, Don Biasone introduced a rule to basketball to speed up the game and bring more excitement. What did he introduce?

(669) Domingo Ghirardelli, founder of the chocolate company that bears his name, came to the United States not to make chocolates, but to do something completely different. When this venture did not "pan" out, he turned to making chocolates. For what reason did he come to America, specifically California?

(670) What distinction does Onorio Razzolini hold in regards to American politics?

(671) What are the top five cities in the United States with the most Americans of Italian decent?

(672) Hank Luisetti, a three-time All-American basketball player at Stanford University during the 1930s pioneered the jump shot. Which other type of basketball shot did he introduce?

TOP 10 OF ITALY
Lowest Population Growth

	REGION	RATE
1	Liguria	-6.7%
2	Friuli-Venezia Giulia	-4.8%
3	Tuscany	-4.0%
4	Emilia-Romagna	-4.0%
5	Piedmont	-3.4%
6	Umbria	-3.3%
7	Marches	-2.3%
8	Molise	-2.3%
9	Valle d'Aosta	-2.2%
10	Abruzzo	-1.3%

Annual Growth Rate

(673) This street is the heart of New York City's Little Italy due to its proximity to the dock where Italian immigrants were ferried from Ellis Island. Name this street.

(674) In New York City you can find a statue of a famous Italian leader in Washington Square. The statue was erected to celebrate the contributions that Italians made during the American Civil War. Name the Italian who is immortalized by the statue.

(675) Joe DiMaggio was not the only person in his family to become an All-Star professional baseball player. Name his two brothers who also accomplished this feat.

(676) Based in New Orleans, Louisiana, this publication was established in 1973 by Joseph Maselli as the "Italian American Voice of the South". Published quarterly, issues contain news and stories on Italian history, genealogy, language, current events and general interest. Name this publication.

(677) Only one person in New York City's history succeeded in defeating the mayoral nominees of both the Democratic and Republican parties. This person ran on the Experience Party ticket in 1949. Name this Palermo-born mayor.

(678) Born Alfred Arnold Cocozza in Philadelphia, this Italian American singer was called "Voice of the Century" by *Time* magazine. In addition, this singer was the first classical artist to sell a million copies of a single album, *Be my Love*, released by RCA. Name him.

(679) This woman was not only the first woman elected governor (Connecticut in 1974), but also the first Italian American woman elected to U.S. Congress. Name her.

(680) Honoring early Italian immigrants from southern Italy, this street is the former 164th Street in Jamaica, New York. Name this former street.

(681) What was the single biggest year of Italian immigration to the United States?

(682) Which acclaimed actor starred in the movies *Apocalypse Now*, *The Freshman* and *The Godfather*, the movie that earned him an Academy Award?

(683) Which Italian American was named the head football coach for the Detroit Lions in 2006 and which Italian American football coach did he replace?

(684) Which young singer from the 1970s performed under the stage name Johnny Baron?

(685) Before 1890, most Italians coming to America were not seeking a permanent home. What were they seeking?

(686) The National Origins Act of 1924 established limits on the number of immigrants that were allowed to enter the United States each year. The result of which was a drastic reduction in the number of Italians immigrating to America. What annual quota was placed on Italian immigration?

(687) What was the late Bobby Darin's birth name?

(688) Which Italian American conductor from New York City received the 1985 Stokowski Award for best conductor?

(689) The "Columbus Doors" depict scenes from the life of Christopher Columbus. Where are these doors located?

(690) Established in 1908 by Florentine Gabriello Spini, this Italian American newspaper is headquartered in Sun Valley, California. Published by Robert Barbera and operated by a foundation bearing the same name, this newspaper has 95 years of service to the Italian American community. Name this newspaper edited by Mario Trecco.

(691) Born Vito Rocco Farinola, this singer was once described by Frank Sinatra as the world's greatest singer. Name this Italian American.

(692) Name the successful businessman who not only established the National Italian American Foundation, but also started both the Chun King company, a provider of canned Chinese food, and Jeno's Inc, a maker of frozen pizzas.

(693) Which month of the year is Italian American Heritage Month celebrated?

(694) Although this American rock star, nicknamed "The Boss", is sometimes mistakenly thought of as Jewish, he is actually of Italian decent. Name him. (Hint: *Born in the U.S.A.*)

(695) Which American pianist, half Swedish and half Italian, became the first American to win the International Chopin Piano Competition in 1970?

(696) For what was Al Capone convicted of and subsequently sentenced to prison?

(697) What is first ethnic Italian Catholic parish, established in 1886, located in the city of Chicago?

(698) In 1955, a bronze bust of Felix Pedro, born Felice Pedroni, was erected in his honor on the campus of the University of Alaska. For what is Pedroni known?

(699) Where was the famous film director Francis Ford Coppola born in America?

(700) What do the *La Sentinella*, *La Nuova Napoli*, *Il Popolo* and *Corriere di Rochester* have in common?

(701) This woman was the 1984 Female Athlete of the Year and became the first female gymnast and youngest athlete to be inducted in the Olympic Hall of Fame in 1990. Name her.

(702) The first use of "Columbus Day" language in America was celebrated in 1869 in which city? (a) San Francisco (b) New York City (c) Baltimore (d) New Orleans

(703) Terrance Gene Bollea is the birth name of Hulk Hogan. What was his profession?

(704) This newspaper, established in 1931 and currently published by former New Jersey State Assemblyman A.J. "Buddy" Fortunato, is one of the largest publications serving and supporting members of the Italian American community and the link to their heritage. Name this very popular weekly newspaper with headquarters in Montclair, New Jersey.

IT HAPPENED IN...535 A.D.

▶Belisarius, chief commander of the Byzantine army, lands in Sicily. From there he attempts to claim the entire Italian peninsula for Byzantine Emperor Justinian I. By 540 Belisarius has taken Ravenna from the Ostrogoths.

(705) Born Ernes Effron Borgnino in 1962, this Italian American starred in such movies as *From Here to Eternity* and *Bad Day at Black Rock*. In 1956, he won a Best Actor Oscar for the movie *Marty*. Name this actor.

(706) Which Italian American female singer of the 1980s was the first ever to have four top hit songs from the same album? (Hint: red-haired punk rocker)

(707) Which Italian American comedian is the host of the NBC *Tonight Show*?

(708) Which Italian American singer and former mayor of Palm Springs, California wrote and sang the hit song *I Got You, Babe* with wife Cher?

(709) Established in 1917 by Italian American Antonio Pasin, this company produces recognizable red colored wagons, previously called Liberty Wagons. Name this company.

(710) Which seemingly unbreakable Major League Baseball single-season record does Joe DiMaggio hold?

(711) Suzette Charles, born Suzette De Gaetano, was the first Italian American to win what title? (a) Miss America (b) top female singer (c) best supporting actress

(712) This complex, located in Washington D.C. and built by an Italian company, was the center of a huge political scandal during the 1970s that culminated in the resignation of President Nixon. Name this complex.

(713) Founded as New Amstel, this city in Delaware was established in 1657 by Italian immigrants. Name this modern city.

(714) Between 1880 and 1900, approximately 9.5 million immigrants arrived in the United States. Approximately how many were from Italy?

(715) What do the Christopher Columbus, Andrea Doria and John Cabot have in common?

(716) Founded in 1950 by Margaret Giannini, M.D. in New York City, this institution was the first in the world to serve the needs of the handicapped. What type of institution did she establish?

(717) Bruno Sammartino, an immigrant to the U.S. from Italy after World War II, suffered from malnutrition when he arrived in America. Soon thereafter he became a professional in this sport and rose to world champion for twelve straight years. Name this sport. (a) wrestling (b) boxing (c) bocce

(718) In which American city can you find the oldest and most famous "Little Italy"?

(719) Which Italian American was the youngest semi-finalist winner at the French Open and the youngest to win a match at Wimbledon?

(720) Mike Eruzione was the captain of this underdog 1980 Olympic team that won the gold medal at Lake Placid, New York by beating the mighty Russian team. Name this Olympic team.

(721) Rhode Island has the highest concentration of Italian Americans as a percentage of the total state population of any state. Which state has the lowest concentration at 0.8%?

(722) Italian American Leonard Riggio, included in the Forbes 400 list of "America's Top CEOs", founded a mega-bookstore chain that has become one of the two leading bookstores in the country. What mega-bookstore chain did he establish?

> **IT HAPPENED IN... 1309 A.D.**
>
> ▶ **Pope Clement V (1305 – 14) moves the papacy from Rome to Avignon, then part of the Kingdom of Naples. This initiated the period of French domination of papal politics, which lasts until 1378.**

(723) Which saint is honored at the oldest Sicilian festival in the United States held in Brooklyn, New York?

(724) Who were the two Italian American members of the "Rat Pack"?

(725) In 1887, this person became the first Italian American elected to the United States Congress. His district included part of Long Island in New York State. Name him.

(726) Which Italian American quarterback from the University of Notre Dame won the Heisman Trophy in 1943 and led the Fighting Irish to a national title in the same year?

(727) Frederic Auguste Bertholdi, sculptor of the Statue of Liberty, created a statue of which Italian explorer that today stands in Providence, Rhode Island?

(728) This Italian American NFL quarterback passed for an astonishing 47 touchdown passes in his first twenty games as a professional football player. Name this now retired quarterback who played for the Miami Dolphins.

(729) From what symbol does the great Seal of the United States originate?

(730) In 1972, Michael Renzulli purchased a company with six stores in New Orleans and turned this company into a beauty supply powerhouse. Name this company.

(731) During the great period of Italian immigration to America, which Italian port was the largest point of departure for Italians leaving for America?

(732) This 3rd century saint not only is the patron saint of Christian music and the patron saint of the blind, but also is the inventor of the organ. Name this saint.

(733) Which Italian American actor hit the big-time as Vinnie Barbarino in the television show *Welcome Back Kotter* and starred as the leading male characters in the movies *Saturday Night Fever* and the original *Grease*?

(734) What do William Paca and Caesar Rodney, both of Italian heritage, have in common? (Hint: 18th century colonial America)

(735) In 1945, a small force of Filipino and American Army Rangers, commanded by Italian American Army colonel Henry A. Mucci, a West Point graduate, went behind enemy lines and rescued the survivors of what infamous death march conducted by the Japanese in 1942?

(736) Born Anthony Dominick Benedetto in Astoria, Queens (New York) in 1926, I am a famous singer who was discovered by Bob Hope in 1949. I am most recognized for my rendition of *I Left My Heart in San Francisco*. Who am I?

(737) Who wrote the *Godfather* and *Superman* movies?

(738) She is one of the leading financial journalists and practically recognizable in all circles. She began her CNBC career in 1995 as the first journalist to report live from the floor of the New York Stock Exchange. Since that time, this New York University educated Italian American has risen to the top. Name this award winning journalist.

(739) In which notorious prison in California did Al Capone serve his sentence after being convicted?

(740) Born in Detroit, Michigan on April 7, 1939, I am most known for my directing of the *Godfather* movies. Who am I?

(741) Of the top ten U.S. cities with the highest number of Italian Americans, eight are located east of the Mississippi River. Name the two cities that are located west of the Mississippi River.

(742) Which movie character did Carlo Rambaldi create that became an instant American hit? (Hint: extraterrestrial)

(743) Paolo Busti, born in Milan in the 18th century, founded what city located on Lake Ontario in New York State?

(744) Who was called "the Michelangelo of the U.S. capitol" for his work on many frescos and paintings for the capitol building?

(745) This company is one of the largest shippers of fresh fruit in the world. Name the brothers who established this company that bears their last name.

(746) Which screenwriter and producer created *The Untouchables*, the film starring Robert De Niro as Al Capone?

(747) At which university was very the first Alpha Phi Delta Italian American fraternity founded in 1914?

(748) Italian immigrant Ettore Boiardi established a company that rose to become the largest supplier of rations to the United States and allied armed forces during World War II. Today, this company specializes in ready-to-eat spaghetti dinners, pasta, and pizza. Name this company.

(749) After whom is New York's LaGuardia airport so named?

(750) Italian American Michael A. Musmanno, a Pennsylvania Supreme Court judge, served on which war crimes tribunal after World War II that tried Nazi war criminals?

(751) American John Howard Payne popularized the expression "Home Sweet Home". How was this expression inspired by Italians?

(752) In 1788, Tuscan-born Filippo Mazzei (Philip Mazzei) wrote the four volume work, *Studies of the Historical and Political Origins of the United States of North America*. In addition, the *Declaration of Independence* incorporated what profound political position of Mazzei that was quoted in 1774 in the *Virginia Gazette*?

(753) This newspaper, established as an Italian language newspaper in 1909 by Italian immigrant Vincent Giuliano, began as *La Tribuna Italiana del Michigan*. Today, this mostly English language newspaper serves both the Detroit and Windsor, Canada metro areas promoting Italian and Italian American heritage. Name this newspaper.

(754) Opened in 1964, this bridge in New York City is one of the longest suspension bridges in the world and is named for the Italian explorer who became the first European to explore New York. Name this bridge.

(755) By what name did Italians refer to Ellis Island?

(756) This Italian American television journalist is the voice of the fixed-income market on the financial network station CNBC. Name this person who began broadcasting from the floor of the Chicago Board of Trade for CNBC in 1999.

(757) Born in Manhattan on August 17, 1943, I am known as an outstanding actor who starred in such movies as *Awakenings*, *The Untouchables*, *Analyze This*, *Goodfellas* and *The Godfather, Part 2*, the movie for which I won an Academy Award. Who am I?

(758) In which 20th century war did over 1,500,000 Italian Americans serve in the U.S. military, thus accounting for 10% of the total American manpower?

(759) This Italian American baseball manager holds the second longest tenure - player, scout, manager and vice president - in baseball history with the same team. During this time, he won five division titles and one World Series championship. Name this manager.

TOP 10 OF ITALY
Most Italians by Country

	COUNTRY	POPULATION
1	Italy	58,800,000
2	U.S.A.	26,000,000
3	Brazil	22,500,000
4	Argentina	13,000,000
5	Venezuela	1,550,000
6	Uruguay	1,500,000
7	Canada	1,270,000
8	France	1,000,000
9	Australia	800,000
10	Switzerland	750,000

(760) Who was the leading Italian American actor of the award-winning television show *M*A*S*H*?

(761) Founded by Dr. Vincenzo Sellaro in 1905, this organization started as a fraternal insurance association. Today, this organization is the largest Italian American organization in the United States and boasts over 2,500 clubs or lodges throughout the country. Name this organization with a lion for a logo.

(762) What is the name of the Italian section in Pittsburgh?

(763) What is the name of the fresco, painted by an Italian American, on the capitol dome?

(764) The first recorded event in the U.S. honoring Columbus and his discovery was held in New York City. This event was organized by the Society of Saint Tammany, or Colombian Order. In which year was this event held? (a) 1723 (b) 1750 (c) 1792

(765) Which Italian American club sponsors one of the oldest continuing footraces in America, held in June since 1918, called the Statuto Race?

(766) Name the fast-food pizzeria, typically found in many shopping malls, that was established by an Italian American bearing his last name.

(767) This Italian American is the past chairman of the National Italian American Foundation. Since 1946, he is the owner and president of a food service and dining equipment company located in Detroit that bears his name. In addition, he was appointed to the Commission for White House Fellows by President Ronald Reagan in 1983. Name this highly-respected person.

(768) Italian American Frank Frazetta was the artist and illustrator of *Tarzan* and *Flash Gordon*. What other television show did he work on? (Hint: set in a future post-nuclear holocaust earth)

(769) Born in the Bronx on April 25, 1940, I am known for such starring roles as Michael Corleone in all three *Godfather* movies and for performances in *Scent of a Woman*, *Carlito's Way*, *Scarface*, and *Heat*. Interestingly, my grandparents originated from Corleone, Sicily. Who am I?

(770) Actor Al Pacino won both an Academy Award and Golden Globe for his performance in which 1992 movie?

(771) Which two states in the U.S. have the highest percentage of Italian Americans?

(772) Charles Bonaparte founded which United States governmental agency in 1908?

(773) Which prestigious university in Washington State was founded by an Italian Jesuit priest in 1881?

(774) Founded by an Italian American in Modesto, California in 1933, this winery not only supplies about 30% of the wine consumed in the United States, but also is the largest producer of wine in the world. Name this company.

(775) Attitio Piccirilli and his five brothers carved which famous landmark and memorial in Washington, D.C.?

(776) Born in 1912, Perry Como was a popular singer who often went by the name "Mr. C". Prior to stardom, what did he do for a living as a young man?

(777) Dr. Robert Gallo, an Italian American virologist and research scientist, co-discovered which deadly virus in 1984?

(778) Which Italian composer is remembered by a statue in Fairmount Park, Philadelphia?

(779) What is the name for the Italian American community in Boston?

(780) General Carl Vuono, appointed by President Ronald Regan, was the first Italian American to serve in what top military capacity?

IT HAPPENED IN...743 B.C.

▶ Corinthians from Greece establish the colony of Syracusae (modern Syracuse) in Sicily. Syracuse will eventually rival Athens as the largest, most powerful and most beautiful city in Greek civilization.

(781) Who was the first American of Italian heritage to run for president of the United States?

(782) During the great period of Italian immigration between 1870 and 1920, nearly four million Italians immigrated to America. Approximately what percentage of the immigrants were from southern Italy?

(783) This Italian market, located in Livonia, Michigan, is consistently voted one of the top Italian markets in the Detroit metro area. Name this market owned and operated by the Fallone family.

(784) Born on June 11, 1913, this longtime Green Bay Packers football coach won five championships and is considered by many to be the greatest football coach of all time. Who is he?

(785) What do college quarterbacks Gino Torreta and Vinny Testaverde share in common?

(786) Which N.A.S.A. space program did Dr. Rocco Petrone direct?

(787) Numerous Italian Americans have received the distinguished U.S. Congressional Medal of Honor for their bravery in battle. Name the three wars with the most Italian Americans having earned this distinction.

(788) Constantino Brumidi painted the mural, *The Apotheosis*, in the dome of which American landmark?

(789) Gennaro Lonbardi, an Italian immigrant from Naples, is credited with establishing the first pizzeria in America. Where did he open his pizzeria?

(790) Most immigrants, including Italian immigrants, arriving in America were received and processed on Ellis Island. In what year did Ellis Island open?

(791) During World War II, Rosie Bonavita was an icon of sorts and a symbol of American women who worked in the factories while men were away in the armed forces. By which other name was she known?

(792) Which Italian built the first nuclear reactor at the University of Chicago to produce power?

(793) Italian scientist and immigrant, Enrico Fermi, was a member of an American team that developed the first atomic bomb. What was the name of their top secret project?

(794) Sylvester Stallone wrote the *Rocky* screenplay and insisted that he act in the leading role. What was the nickname for his character in the *Rocky* movies?

(795) This U.S. Senator, born on March 25, 1958 in Roseville, California, was named 2005 Legislator of the Year by the Humane Society of the United States for his commitment to the humane treatment of animals. Name this Nevada senator of Tuscan heritage who was elected in 2000.

(796) Italian American Francis Rogallo is credited with developing a type of personal flying invention made of woven metal covered by a silicon base. What did he invent in 1948?

(797) Commissioned by the United States government after the War of American Independence, what American symbol did Giuseppe Franzoni sculpt?

(798) He played the character of Lieutenant Dan Taylor in the movie *Forrest Gump* and also starred in *Reindeer Games*. Who is this Italian American actor?

(799) At which university did the Italian American music star and entertainer Madonna study dance?

(800) Born in Martinez, California on November 25, 1914, I am known as one of the greatest baseball players of all time and most remembered for my record for the longest number of games with a hit. I had a .325 lifetime average and led the American league in batting average in 1939 and 1940. Who am I?

(801) Which actor won an Academy Award for Best Supporting Actor as Don Vito Corleone in *The Godfather, Part II*?

IT HAPPENED IN...1436 A.D.

▶ **The Duomo in Florence is finished and consecrated. This event signals a new era as this dome is the first large-scale dome erected in Christian Europe since the fall of the Roman Empire.**

(802) What is the Italian section of Saint Louis called?

(803) Italian American Phil Rizzuto, nicknamed "The Scooter", was the popular voice of which Major League Baseball team?

(804) Which college was the first in America to offer Italian language instruction? (Hint: located in Virginia)

(805) Name the head coach of the Penn State University football team.

(806) Which fruit packaging company, founded in Florida by Anthony Rossi in 1947, is today the largest producer and marketer of fruit juices in the world?

(807) Born Angelo Siciliano in Calabria, this Italian American bodybuilder immigrated with his family to America in 1904. He created the bodybuilding technique called isometrics and was referred to as the "World's Most Perfectly Developed Man". Name him.

(808) Where does Italian rank in the "top ten largest ethnic groups" in the United States?

(809) In what 1953 film did Jerry Lewis and Dean Martin immortalize the song *That's Amore*?

(810) This U.S. Senator, born in 1958 and raised in Butler County, Pennsylvania, is the son of an Italian immigrant from Riva del Garda, Trentino-Alto Adige. On January 4, 1995, this senator was sworn-in as a United States Senator from Pennsylvania. He was just 35 years old at the time. Name this senator.

(811) What is the origin of the derogatory term "Wop"?

(812) In 1970, Francis Ford Coppola won an Oscar for best original story and screenplay about a legendary World War II American general and tank commander. This same film was nominated for Best Picture of the year. Name this film starring George C. Scott.

(813) This well-respected and highly successful Italian American coached men's basketball at the University of Kentucky, Boston Celtics and is presently the head coach at the University of Louisville. Name this distinguished coach.

(814) One of the first novels to portray the Italian American experience was written by Pietro DiDonato. What is the title of this novel?

(815) How many Italian Americans served as U.S. Senators and U.S. House of Representatives during 2003 to 2005?

(816) What is the "Little Italy" section of Philadelphia called?

(817) Born Concetta Franconero in 1938, this Italian American music star sung such hits as *Who's Sorry Now* and *Where the Boys Are* (1963). Name her.

(818) This Italian American, a graduate of Georgetown University and Harvard Law, is the first American of Italian heritage to serve on the United States Supreme Court. Name him.

(819) George Randazzo, a Chicago businessman, created a sports organization and museum in 1978 to honor the contributions Italian Americans have made to athletics. Name this organization and museum located in Chicago.

(820) Which American singer was born Frank Paul Lo Vecchio?

(821) What is the name for the center of the Italian community in Chicago located just west of the loop?

(822) Which two great leaders of the American Revolution were fluent in Italian?

(823) This U.S. Senator, born on May 7, 1932 in Albuquerque, New Mexico, is one of five children of Italian immigrants from Lucca, Tuscany. He is also the first Republican in 38 years elected from New Mexico to the United States Senate. Name this senator.

(824) In contrast to the immigration boom of 1880 to 1930, the 30-year period of 1820 to 1850 saw approximately how many Italians immigrate to America?

(825) New Yorker Francis B. Spinola was the very first Italian American to serve in which political establishment?

(826) In 1837, Italian American John Phinizy became the first Italian American mayor of a major U.S. city. Name this city. (a) Providence, Rhode Island (b) Washington, D.C. (c) Augusta, Georgia

(827) Which actor, turned director, was born Carole Penny Masciarelli?

(828) Born in Los Angeles in 1954, this Italian American actor starred in such movies as *Tin Cup*, *The Thomas Crown Affair*, and *Major League*. Name her.

(829) In 1981, this baseball player won the Cy Young Award for his outstanding relief pitching. Who is this pitcher that sports a trademark mustache? (Hint: hands and fingers)

(830) Born in Lercara Friddi on November 24, 1897, I am known as the most powerful crime boss in American history. Who am I?

(831) The Garibaldi-Meucci Museum is dedicated to two Italians - father of Italian unification and inventor of the telephone. Both of these Italians lived in the U.S. during the 19th century. In which American city can you find this museum?

(832) The Cathedral of Saints Peter and Paul in Philadelphia was modeled after a church in Rome. After which church in Rome was the cathedral modeled?

(833) Between 1901 and 1910, about how many Italians immigrated to the United States?

(834) Who performed the introductory music at the April 22, 1964 World's Fair in New York City?

(835) Awarded the Medal of Honor for his bravery, General Luigi Palma di Cesnola was one of four native Italian generals to serve in the United States Army. In which war did he fight?

(836) Where in the United States can you find a desk used by Christopher Columbus and the cross he used to claim territory in the New World for Spain?

(837) In 1968, Columbus Day was declared a federal public holiday by President Lyndon B. Johnson. This day is celebrated every year on one day during the month of October. Which day is Columbus Day held?

TOP 10 OF ITALY

Italian Americans by State

	STATE	POPULATION
1	New York	2,890,408
2	New Jersey	1,590,225
3	Pennsylvania	1,547,470
4	California	1,533,599
5	Florida	1,147,946
6	Massachusetts	918,838
7	Illinois	739,284
8	Ohio	720,847
9	Connecticut	652,016
10	Michigan	484,486

(838) Which city in upstate New York is named after a city in Sicily that was founded by the ancient Greeks?

(839) Which classic television cartoon characters were invented by Italian Americans?

(840) The first sizeable group of Italian immigrants to America arrived in 1657 from Holland. This group settled in the Dutch colonies of New Amsterdam (now New York) and founded New Castle in Delaware. Who were these first Italian immigrants to America?

(841) What flamboyant Italian American grand piano entertainer was born in Wisconsin, starred in the movie *Sincerely Yours*, and became an icon in the 20th century?

(842) Al Martino, who played the role of Johnny Fontaine in *The Godfather*, hit the big-time with what song? (Hint: look to Spain)

(843) What was Frank Sinatra's first hit record?

IT HAPPENED IN...1480 A.D.

► **The town of Otranto is attacked by a Turkish fleet with the help of Venetians. After the conquest, only 800 inhabitants remained living. When these people refused to convert to Islam, they were executed. The executioner converts to Christianity and is executed.**

---

(844) Name the prestigious and acclaimed tennis school, named for its founder, located in Bradenton, Florida.

(845) Which Italian American architect is considered by many to be the father of post-modernism architecture?

(846) The first monument to Christopher Columbus was dedicated on October 12, 1792 to honor the 300th anniversary of the discovery of America. Where was this first monument erected?

(847) In 1999, the median national income was $50,000 per year. What was it for Italian Americans? (a) $45,200 (b) $47,500 (c) $55,100 (d) $61,300

(848) Born in Knoxville, Tennessee in 1963, this dual director and actor directed the movies *Reservoir Dogs*, *True Romance* and *Pulp Fiction*, the film that won him an Oscar. Name him.

---

(849) Conductor and composer Bill Conti received an Academy Award in 1983 for the music to what hit movie about the early American space flight program?

(850) This person, the son of an Italian immigrant, was the highest-ranking Italian American naval officer to serve during the Civil War. In 1887, he became commander-in-chief of the North Atlantic Squadron. Name him.

(851) The expression "E Pluribus Unum", imprinted on the currency of the United States of America, was originally written by the great Roman poet Horace (Quintus Horatius Flaccus) in his work entitled *Epistles Book II*. What does this expression mean in Latin?

(852) Which celebration in the United States resembles Carnevale?

(853) Italian American Willie Mosconi, who once made 526 shots without an error, was world champion fifteen straight years in the 1940s and 1950s. Name this sport. (a) darts (b) bocce (c) billiards

(854) What is the historical significance of the Saint Mary Magdalene de Pazzi Church, established in Philadelphia in 1852?

(855) Born on June 18, 1913 in Minnesota, I graduated from Stanford University in 1937 with a degree in economics and business administration and worked for my father at his winery. Thereafter, I established a California winery that has become one of the most successful wineries in the world. Who am I?

(856) Why was the town of Rome, Georgia named after the city of Rome in Italy?

(857) Name the actor and mother of Italian American Liza Minnelli. (Hint: *Wizard of Oz*)

(858) Which Italian American family was once the leading investor in sports enterprises and held a significant level of influence on professional sports?

(859) Italian American Generoso Pope, Jr. established which popular tabloid newspaper?

(860) Born in Bisaquino on May 18, 1897, I am known for my directing, including such movies as *It's a Wonderful Life* and *Mr. Smith Goes to Washington*, the movie for which I received an Oscar for Best Director. Who am I?

(861) This author and traveler, after whom a county in Minnesota is named, was an early explorer who discovered the source of the Mississippi River in 1823. Name him.

(862) Which movie of Italian American life, released during the 1980s, starred Nicholas Cage and singer Cher?

(863) Italian American Bill Paternostro created what famous landmarks in the sidewalks of Hollywood?

(864) Elected to the Baseball Hall of Fame in 1972, I was named the American League's Most Valuable Player three times (1951, 1954, and 1955) and played in 16 All Star games. Who am I?

(865) James Delligatti is credited with inventing what tremendously successful fast-food sandwich? (Hint: yellow arches)

(866) Which actor played Archie Bunker's Italian next door neighbor in the television series *All in the Family*?

(867) What event inspired the mother of Italian American superstar actor Leonardo DiCaprio, while pregnant with him, to give him the first name of Leonardo?

(868) Which U.S. state has the highest number of Italian American residents?

(869) According to U.S. Census Bureau reports, approximately how many people of Italian heritage reside in the United States?

(870) Born Alicia Augello Clark in 1981 in New York City, this Italian American won five Grammy Awards in 2001 for her song, *Fallin*. Name her.

(871) Born in San Jose, California on May 6, 1870, I founded the private Bank of Italy, which today is known as Bank of America. Who am I?

(872) How many Italians served in the American Continental Army during the War of American Independence?

(873) In 1985, this Italian American actor won an Academy Award for Best Supporting Actor for the movie *Cocoon*. His other roles include *Trading Places* and *Coming to America*. Name him.

(874) Italian American Tony LaRussa received what Major League Baseball honor three times since 1983?

(875) How many Italian Americans received the highest medals of honor for military bravery during World War II?

(876) Born in Allentown, Pennsylvania on October 15, 1924, I am known for my staggering turnaround of Chrysler Corporation in the early 1980s and was known as the "King of Detroit". Who am I?

(877) Born in Lombardy in 1850, this person became an American citizen in 1909 and became the first American saint when canonized by Pope Pius XII on July 7, 1946. Name this first American saint.

(878) Which university in New Jersey was founded by an Italian American in 1942?

(879) What turbulent event of the 20th century caused many Italian Americans to stop teaching their children the Italian language?

(880) Who created the cartoon characters and television programs *Tom & Jerry*, *Scooby-Doo*, *Flintstones* and *Smurfs*?

(881) The American *Pledge of Allegiance* was recited publicly for the first time during an event, presided over by President Harrison, honoring the achievements of an Italian. Which Italian did they honor at this event?

(882) This titanic box-office grossing movie is about an ocean liner that sank after hitting an iceberg. Name this movie starring Leonardo DiCaprio.

(883) Which infamous outlaw of the 19th century was captured by Italian American Angelo Siringo?

(884) Name the famous boxer who once said, "It was the saddest punch of my life", referring to the knock-out punch to Joe Louis in 1951.

(885) Of the four mega popular Italian American singers of the 20th century - Frank Sinatra, Dean Martin, Tony Bennett, and Perry Como - who produced the most hit songs?

(886) This actor, the descendant of Italian Protestants from Italy by way of Holland in the 17th century, starred in many Hollywood movies, including *Midway* and *On Golden Pond*, the 1981 movie that landed him an Academy Award for Best Actor. Name this Italian American.

(887) Who was the first European to proclaim the splendor of Niagara Falls in the early 17th century?

(888) What was the name of the Union Army unit, named for a leading Italian military figure of the time, composed mainly of Italians during the American Civil War?

(889) Which boxer was called "The Rock" and the "Brockton Blockbuster"?

(890) Which Italian American actor, born in Huntington, New York, starred in the *Karate Kid* movies?

(891) Nicknamed Nappy, Dominic Napolitano was a head coach at the University of Notre Dame for over fifty years. What sport did he coach?

(892) Born in Brooklyn in 1944, I am known for my leadership as New York's mayor when terrorists struck the World Trade Center in 2001. Who am I?

(893) What is the birth name of Madonna, the renowned musician and entertainer, born in Bay City, Michigan on August 16, 1958?

TOP 10 OF ITALY

Top Regions for Emigration

	REGION	%	EMIGRANTS
1	Calabria	0.24%	4,898
2	Basilicata	0.16%	972
3	Sicily	0.16%	7,785
4	Friuli Venezia Giulia	0.14%	1,738
5	Trentino-Alto Adige	0.13%	1,311
6	Molise	0.13%	425
7	Veneto	0.13%	5,907
8	Liguria	0.11%	1,820
9	Lombardy	0.11%	10,006
10	Lazio	0.11%	5,560

Ranked by % of Total Region Population

(894) Which major American Midwestern city, once called the Paris of the Midwest, was co-founded by an Italian in 1704?

(895) In 1805, President Thomas Jefferson recruited musicians from Italy to organize a permanent United States Marine Band. From which region did the musicians originate?

(896) Which university did two Italian Jesuit priests establish in the bay area of California in 1851?

(897) What was the name of the quartet in which Frank Sinatra sang and performed as a teenager?

(898) Matt Biondi is tied for being the most decorated U.S. Olympian in history with 11 medals (8 golds, 2 silvers, and 1 bronze). In what sport did he compete?

(899) What disease, rampant in southern Italy in the late-19th century, motivated many Italians to leave for America?

(900) What is the name for the Italian American section of Providence, Rhode Island?

(901) Confirmed by the U.S. Senate in 2006, who became the second Italian American to serve on the United States Supreme Court?

(902) Which Italian American baseball player said, "It's deja vu all over again" and "It's difficult to make predictions, especially about the future"?

CHAPTER E·I·G·H·T VIII

LANGUAGE, LITERATURE, & PHILOSOPHY

Investigating Italian Communication and Expression

"Know how to listen, and you will profit even from those who talk badly."

- PLUTARCH

"Nothing strengthens authority so much as silence."

- LEONARDO DA VINCI

(903) This commonly spoken English word originated from an Italian word meaning a musical composition or performance accomplished by an individual voice or instrument. What is this Italian word?

(904) This commonly spoken English word originated from a Latin word referring to the sand spread on the ground after gladiatorial fights to soak up blood. What is this Latin word?

(905) The word for the common "flu", which some believed was caused by the influence of the stars, is derived from what Italian word?

(906) Which literary greats are known as the "Tuscany Trinity" for their attempt to reconcile the classical tradition of the ancient Romans and Greeks with Christianity?

(907) Name the dialect in Italy that is a combination of Italian and Hebrew.

(908) What does the Italian expression "La Dolce Vita" mean in English?

(909) The ancient Etruscan language used the Euboean Greek alphabet, which itself is partly derived from Phoenician letters. Today, how much of the ancient Etruscan writings are we able to read and understand?

(910) Where does the Latin alphabet rank among the most widely used alphabetic writing systems in the world?

(911) Who is considered the counterpart of William Shakespeare in Italy?

(912) Which region of Italy did Italian literary greats Dante and Petrarch (Francesco Patrarch) say gave birth to poetry?

(913) This commonly spoken English word originated from an Italian word meaning a grand show or event. What is this Italian word?

(914) Greek is an officially recognized minority language of Italy. Which two regions have the largest concentrations of Greek speaking people?

(915) Although the Tuscan dialect is the standard tongue in Italy, which other Italian dialect is gaining in usage?

(916) What is the French word for the Italian word "ancora" and what does this word mean in English?

(917) Name the admired fairytales introduced by Italian authors Gianbattista Basile, Carlo Collodi, Giovanni Boccaccio, and Giovanni Francesco Straparola.

(918) Translate the Italian proverb "Lontano dagli occhi, lontano dal cuore".

(919) This commonly spoken English word originated from an Italian word meaning stretched fabric over a collapsible hinged rib. What is this Italian word? (Hint: contraption used in the rain and at the beach)

(920) Approximately what percentage of Italians only speak their native Italian language and no foreign language?

(921) According to some estimates, what percentage of English words originated from the Latin language?

(922) Bearing a Latin name, what is the greatest document in English history?

(923) Which of the Nobel Prize categories - chemistry, literature, physics, peace, economics and medicine - boasts the most Italian recipients?

(924) Born in Arezzo on July 20, 1511, I am known for building the Uffizi in Florence and for my acclaimed book, *The Lives of the Most Eminent Painters, Sculptors and Architects*, in 1550. Who am I?

(925) This commonly spoken English word originated from an Italian word meaning a place where artisans work. What is this Italian word?

(926) Nobel Prizes were awarded to Italians Luigi Pirandello and Dario Fo, a playwright awarded in 1997. In what category were they so awarded?

(927) The English word "cash" originated from a Latin word meaning "money box". Name this Latin word.

(928) Dante's timeless literary work, *The Divine Comedy*, was not originally given that title. The title was changed nearly two hundred years after his death. What did Dante originally title his work?

(929) What is the significance of "23 Via Capello" in the town of Verona? (Hint: Capelletti and Montecchi)

(930) In which Italian city did the first public library open to the world in 1571?

(931) What are the five Romance languages and which is considered the most difficult to master?

(932) What Latin word, sometimes used in the American legal system as a means of defense, translates to "elsewhere"?

(933) The motto of the United States Marine Corp is a Latin expression. What is this expression?

(934) This commonly spoken English word originated from an Italian word meaning mountain that explodes sending ash and lava into the air. What is this Italian word?

(935) What word, derived from Latin for "I see", is now ingrained in television terminology?

(936) The word "pasta" is derived from what Italian word meaning a combination of flour and water?

(937) This Latin word describes an event best defined as "an observable event on earth that cannot be explained by natural laws". As a result, this event is considered an Act of God by the Catholic Church. Name this word.

(938) What commonly used Latin term means "per person"?

(939) This commonly spoken English word originated from an Italian word meaning a situation at hand, potential occurrences, or possible events that could unfold. What is this Italian word?

(940) Born in Florence in 1265, I am known for my epic poem, *The Divine Comedy*. Who am I?

(941) Alessandro Manzoni (1785 - 1873), considered the greatest writer since the Renaissance, is credited with helping to foster the Tuscan dialect as the modern Italian national language and pushing for Italian unification. Name his 1827 masterpiece book for which he is most remembered.

(942) What is a "chiesa"?

(943) What two Latin abbreviations are commonly used to substitute for the grammatical expressions "that is" and "for example"?

(944) Which Italian word, now commonly used in English as well, means a copy of something?

(945) Today, the word "Ciao" is used informally throughout Italy to say hello and goodbye. Was this always the case?

(946) What does miramar refer to in Italian?

(947) What is the Italian word for Christmas manger?

(948) The Latin abbreviation B.I.D. is commonly used by medical professionals when prescribing medication. What does B.I.D. stand for?

(949) Which Italian word means a situation getting worse or a complete failure?

(950) What is the translation for "Caveat emptor", a common expression used since ancient Roman times?

(951) In Italian, which animal is a gato?

(952) What is the meaning of the Italian proverb "Ama il prossimo tuo come te stesso"?

(953) What do the following Latin words have in common - Lundei, Martedi, Mercoledi, Geovedi, Venerdi, Sabato, and Domenica?

(954) What printing style was invented in Fabriano, Italy in the 13th century that enabled marks to be made to a document without taking up valuable writing space?

(955) What does the word "FINE" signify at the end of an Italian movie?

(956) Boccaccio is known for helping people forget what terrible experience with his humoristic writings?

(957) What does the expression "La Famiglia e Sacra" mean?

(958) The words "Kaiser" in German and "Czar" in Russian originated from which Latin word?

(959) Which Italian word, now commonly used in English as well, means artwork or paintings on a wall, ceiling or floor?

(960) Who was the first person to write in Italian rather than Latin in scientific works?

(961) Latin was the official language for all English governmental and legal documents until what late century when Latin was replaced by English?

(962) Raised in Italy but born in Santiago de las Vegas, Cuba on October 15, 1923, I am known for popular literary works, including the famous collection entitled *The Non-Existent Knight and the Cloven Viscount*. Who am I?

(963) Legendary Greek philosopher Plato once resided for part of his life in which town now located in Italy?

(964) When is the word "prego" commonly used?

(965) This commonly spoken English word originated from an Italian word meaning the magma that flows out of volcanoes. What is this Italian word?

(966) To what does the term Ferragosto, associated with the Feast of the Assumption, refer?

(967) This dialect more closely resembles Latin than any other dialect or language in the world today. It is the standard for official Italian documents, newspapers, radio and television and is the official dialect taught to schoolchildren in Italy. Name this dialect.

(968) Italkim means Italians in what language?

(969) This commonly spoken English word originated from an Italian word meaning a covering of exterior walls. What is this Italian word?

(970) Nicolo and Nicola are both Italian words for Nicholas. Why the difference between the Italian versions?

(971) What does the Italian word "belvedere" translate or refer to?

(972) What is an Italian attempting to accomplish when he says "senta"?

(973) Is "Geghe" a language, a food, or a city descended from Albanians that settled in Italy long ago?

(974) Italian Charles Botta is credited with writing the first history book on this epic 18th century struggle for freedom and self-government. On what subject did he write?

(975) What modern military special forces group derives its name from Italian?

(976) This word in English originated from erratic scribbling or figures on the walls of tombs and catacombs in ancient Rome and Italy. What is this word?

(977) This book, written by Machiavelli over a twenty-year period and condemned by the pope, is about how to govern Italy free from foreign domination. Today, this book is still referenced and is viewed as a book for the politically cunning. Name the title of this book that was published in 1532.

(978) "All Gaul is divided into three parts" is the beginning of the work titled *Commentaries on the Gallic War*. Name the Roman general who wrote this legendary work.

NICCOLO MACCHIAVELLI

(979) This commonly spoken English word originated from an Italian word meaning brightly colored paper traditionally thrown on special Italian days. What is this Italian word?

(980) Before the calendar year acronyms B.C. and A.D. were introduced in the 6th century, the acronym A.U.C. was used. This acronym stood for Anno Urbis Conditae. What does this expression mean in English?

(981) Which English word is derived from the Italian word infanteria?

(982) Giorgio Vascari (1511-1574) is most known for his writing of a landmark multi-volume masterpiece that became the basis of Italian art history. Name the title of his multi-volume work.

(983) This commonly spoken English word originated from an Italian word meaning smuggled or illegal merchandise. What is this Italian word?

(984) Approximately 80% of the people living in this region of Italy are direct descendants of the native people that inhabited the area before the time of the ancient Romans. Their language is the largest officially spoken minority language in Italy. Name the language these people speak.

(985) When someone is called Machiavellian, what type of person are they considered?

(986) What does libretto refer to in the Italian language?

(987) Approximately when did the Latin language develop fixed rules of meaning and grammar?

(988) Julius Caesar was frequently quoted as saying "Veni, Vidi, Vici". This expression was first spoken by Caesar to report his victory over Pharnaces, King of Pontus, in 47 BC. What is the English translation?

(989) This commonly spoken English word originated from an Italian word meaning an expression used to convey something special about a person or organization. What is this Italian word?

(990) The fall of the Roman Empire and the destruction of Rome by the Vandals, a Germanic tribe, inspired what term that is used today to describe destructive acts?

(991) What does an Italian say when he sends you good wishes?

(992) What is the name for the language group that is based on the Latin language?

(993) Dante Alighieri's literary work, *La Divina Commedia* (*The Devine Comedy*), is considered one of the greatest literary works of human history. This work is a trilogy of poems where Latin poet Virgil is the guide through the inferno. What places or settings comprise the trilogy?

(994) This word, now commonplace in English, originated from Latin meaning a large open hall or patio located within a Roman villa. What is this word?

(995) This commonly spoken English word originated from an Italian word meaning an ethnic section of a city or town that is economically depressed. What is this Italian word?

(996) Born in Milan on March 7, 1785, I am known for defining the modern Italian language by rewriting my novel, *Il Promesso Sposi*, with a Tuscan dialect, thus promoting a unified Italy and unified language. Who am I?

(997) The English word "music" is derived from the Italian word "musica", which itself is derived from the word "mousike". From what language does "mousike" originate?

IT HAPPENED IN...1504 A.D.

▶ **Michelangelo completes and unveils in the Piazza della Signoria in Florence his great work, the *David* statue. The statue is made from one large piece of marble from the town of Carrara.**

(998) The ancient Romans typically referred to the Mediterranean Sea as Mare Nostrum. What does this mean in Latin?

(999) Two ways Italians can say goodbye include the words "Arrivederci" and "ArrivederLa". What is the difference between these similar meaning words?

(1000) This commonly spoken English word originated from an Italian word meaning the ending of a musical composition or the closing scene of a performance or production. What is this Italian word?

(1001) What does the word "stinco" mean in the Italian language?

(1002) Born in Paris to Italian parents in 1313, I am considered the father of the psychological novel and the short story. Who am I?

(1003) Triennial is the Latin name used to describe a three year period of elapsed time. What are the Latin names for 50 year and 100 year periods of elapsed time?

CHAPTER 8

CHAPTER
N·I·N·E

MILITARY HISTORY & CONTRIBUTIONS
Pivotal Battles and Wars that Shook the Landscape

"I would rather be first in a little Oberian village than second in Rome."

- JULIUS CAESAR

"Democracy is beautiful in theory; in practice it is a fallacy."

- BENITO MUSSOLINI

(1004) This infamous leader, known as "The Scourge of God", conquered much of Europe and drove Germanic tribes into the Roman Empire for safety, only to see those Germanic tribes conquer the Roman Empire itself. Name him.

(1005) During the Renaissance, mercenaries were hired and fought for the numerous Italian city-states. The city-state of Venice employed 30,000 such mercenaries alone. One of the most popular was a mercenary leader from England, Sir John Hawkwood, who fought for Florence. What was the name given to these soldiers of fortune?

(1006) Which legendary World War II German field marshall, known as the "Desert Fox", was captured by the Italian Army in World War I and held in a prisoner of war camp until his escape?

(1007) This legendary Carthaginian general ravaged the Roman Republic and defeated the Romans in battle on numerous occasions. He was finally defeated outside Carthage at the battle of Zama. While in exile in present-day Turkey, he committed suicide rather than face extradition to Rome and subsequent punishment. Name him.

(1008) What was the name for the list of principles and rules established by Mussolini that "perfect" Fascist militiamen were obligated to follow?

(1009) At the Battle of Actium (31 B.C.), Roman General Gaius Octavian (later Emperor Augustus), defeated what legendary couple to secure Roman control over Egypt?

(1010) This Roman orator and enemy of Roman Emperor Marc Antony, was captured by bounty hunters while attempting to escape Rome. His head and hand were severed and presented to Antony, who then had them placed in the Forum in Rome. Who was this great Roman orator?

(1011) Which small island nation, due south of Sicily, hosted a large British military base during World War II that was used extensively in operations against the Axis powers?

(1012) How many Italian battleships were sunk during Word War II?

(1013) What percentage of Italian Jews were deported to German death camps during World War II?

(1014) This hilltop fortress, located in the Judean desert, was the site of the final Jewish revolt and stronghold against the Romans. Prior to its capture in 73 A.D., the Jews inside the fortress committed suicide rather than face capture and made slaves. Name this hilltop fortress.

(1015) Barracks, post, stockade, ambush, salvo and barricade have what in common?

(1016) During World War II, the United States produced nearly 300,000 aircraft. Approximately how many did Italy produce?

(1017) This large island in the Mediterranean was won by the Romans through a hotly contested war with Carthage in the first Punic War. Once under Roman control, this island became the first province and bread basket of the ancient Roman Republic. Name this island.

TOP 10 OF ITALY
Top Immigrant Destinations

	REGION	%	IMMIGRANTS
1	Lombardy	22.50%	73,405
2	Veneto	11.60%	37,834
3	Lazio	10.90%	35,607
4	Emilia-Romagna	10.00%	32,679
5	Piedmont	8.00%	25,979
6	Tuscany	7.60%	24,693
7	Campania	4.30%	13,843
8	Sicily	3.90%	12,760
9	Marche	3.30%	10,662
10	Liguria	2.60%	8,352

Ranked by % of Total Immigration

(1018) What is the name of the Roman general that defeated Hannibal at Zama, outside of Carthage, in 202 B.C. during the Second Punic War?

(1019) Started by Roman Emperor Trajan around 53 B.C., Pax Romana is the name given to an unprecedented period in Roman history that lasted for 200 years. What was the Pax Romana?

(1020) Established by Roman Emperor Augustus as the imperial bodyguard, this organization quickly gained significant power and rendered some future emperor powerless. What is the name for this "guard" unit that lasted until the reign of Emperor Constantine?

(1021) How many aircraft carriers did Italy operate during World War II?

(1022) The United States was the top country for repatriating Italian prisoners of war at the close of World War II. Which country was the worst with only 14% of prisoners returned?

(1023) This queen of beauty was the last Macedonian ruler of Egypt. She gave birth to one child with Julius Caesar and three children with Marc Antony. Name this queen that met her demise together with Marc Antony.

(1024) What was the salute of the Fascists?

(1025) On June 10, 1940, which two countries did Italy declare war on during the early stage of World War II?

(1026) Caledonia, a land north of the Roman Empire, proved too costly to subdue by the Romans. Hadrian's Wall was built to keep these ferocious people, nicknamed the "Painted People" for the blue coloring they covered their bodies with before going into battle, out of the empire. Name this modern-day land.

(1027) The victory over the Ottoman Turks at the Battle of Lepanto in 1571 signaled the rise of which Italian city-state?

(1028) Italian Giulio Douhet, Undersecretary of Air under Mussolini, wrote a book that advocated the use of air power to employ ground attacks to subdue enemy forces. Which nation was most inspired by this book?

(1029) On May 26, 1805 this French general received the crown of Charlemagne by Pope Pius VII in a Milan cathedral. Name this historical figure crowned King of Italy.

(1030) During the 3rd and 2nd centuries B.C., Rome battled a great power for supremacy of the western Mediterranean. This enemy of Rome was founded by the Phoenicians as a western colony and quickly grew to become powerful in their own right. Name this enemy that the Romans fought in the Punic Wars.

(1031) At the outset of World War II, Italy had one of the world's largest fleets of this type of warship, beginning the war with 117 warships. Name this type of warship.

(1032) During World War II, the capture of what island off the coast of Sicily by the Allied forces in June of 1943 launched the Italian campaign and the beginning of the end for Mussolini?

(1033) This town, called Cassinum by the ancient Romans, is known for its famous Abbey of Monte Cassino, established in A.D. 529. During World War II, this town was devastated in a famous battle that was later depicted on the big screen by Hollywood. Name this town located 80 miles south of Rome.

(1034) The Venetians were the first to mount what type of weapon on naval vessels?

(1035) Approximately how many years did the ancient Romans colonize and occupy modern-day England?

(1036) Invented in Italy in the early 14th century, this weapon was the first cannon that fired iron projectiles. Name this weapon.

(1037) The Saracens (Arabs) were responsible for introducing sugar cane, coffee, cotton, oranges, lemons and other fruit to Europe via their 9th century conquest of Sicily. What people expelled the Saracens for good from Italy in the 11th century?

(1038) Similar to the Blue Angels in America, this elite group of military pilots is trained to represent Italy in special air shows around the world. Name this elite aviation unit.

(1039) Who were considered the most revered, and therefore most expensive, of all ancient Roman slaves?

(1040) During World War II, who were the Partigiani?

(1041) The ancient Romans battled the Gauls of Northern Italy and France on numerous occasions during their history. Today, we know the Gauls by another name. What is that name?

(1042) When did the Italian Army switch from being a compulsory force to a fully-volunteer profession?

(1043) In the early 20th century, Italy regained the territories of Trieste, Istria, Zara and Lagostam from the Austrian-Hungarian Empire following their loss and subsequent break-up. After what major event did this occur?

(1044) During World War II, Radio Bari was used for what purpose?

(1045) What type of ancient Roman warcraft was a quinquereme?

(1046) Saint Francis of Assisi experienced a tragic event in his life that transformed him into the saintly person we know. What nearly year long experience did he endure?

(1047) On July 10, 1943 - during the height of World War II - the allies landed in Italy to liberate the country from Fascist and German control. Where did the allies first land?

(1048) Prior to World War II in the mid-1930s, which European nation did Italy nearly go to war with over the planned annexation of Austria?

(1049) What was the primary difference between a Roman legionnaire and auxiliary?

(1050) Pope Saint Leo persuaded what infamous Hun leader to spare Rome in A.D. 452?

(1051) For what purpose did ancient Roman gladiators use olive oil?

(1052) During World War II, the Germans blew up all bridges across the Arno river in Florence except for one bridge. Name this historically significant bridge.

(1053) What were the three weapons typically carried by a Roman legionnaire?

(1054) How did Mussolini receive his distinct facial scars?

(1055) Name three military ranks that originated in Italy. (Hint: all begin with the letter "C")

> ## IT HAPPENED IN...1571 A.D.
> ▶ At the pivotal battle of Lepanto, a combined Venetian, Spanish and papal fleet destroys the Turkish fleet off the coast of Greece. Turkish naval aggression is forever limited.

(1056) Guido Rossi, an Italian fighter "ace", shot down many Allied planes during World War II. What questionable and dubious method did he employ to accomplish this feat?

(1057) This Roman structure, commissioned by Emperor Hadrian and completed in 126 A.D., is seventy-three miles long, ten feet wide and fifteen feet high in most places. In addition, this structure had guard posts about every two miles. Name this structure that was abandoned by the Romans in A.D. 383.

(1058) In 1930, under order from Benito Mussolini, Italy invaded the nation of Abyssinia located in East Africa. What is the modern name for this nation?

(1059) Occurring on Easter in 1282, Sicilian Vespers is the name for a revolt which occurred in Sicily against foreign occupation. Which foreign occupiers did the people of Sicily revolt against on this day?

(1060) How many legions were in a typical Roman army?

(1061) The Praetorian Guard was responsible for safeguarding Roman emperors. How did this unit acquire its name?

(1062) How many battleships did Italy operate during World War II?

(1063) Approximately how many years did it take the ancient Romans to expand, either by conquest or diplomacy, throughout the Italian peninsula? (a) 112 (b) 210 (c) 600 (d) 900

(1064) During his battles with the Romans in the Punic Wars, Hannibal employed this animal to strike fear and wreck havoc on Roman formations and morale. Pyrrhus from Greece also brought this animal into battle against the Romans. What type of animal did they employ in battle?

(1065) Which European nation did Italy form an alliance with in 1936?

(1066) This was the sacred symbol of the ancient Roman legions that was expected to be defended to the death and, if captured, was a significant disgrace. What was this symbol?

(1067) What event caused the population of Rome to decline from nearly 1,000,000 residents to fewer than 100,000 in A.D. 455?

(1068) What type of naval ship is the Italian Giuseppe Garibaldi?

(1069) The introduction and fighting of gladiators did not originate in ancient Rome. From which civilization did the Romans learn about gladiators?

(1070) Approximately how many captured Italians soldiers were interned in the United States during World War II?

CHAPTER
T · E · N

MUSIC, ART, & ARCHITECTURE

Exploring Italian Masters of Craft

*"Even the richest soil, if left uncultivated,
will produce the rankest weeds."*

- LEONARDO DA VINCI

*"If people only knew how hard I work to gain my mastery,
it wouldn't seem so wonderful at all."*

- MICHELANGELO BUONARROTI

(1071) Which famous Leonardo da Vinci painting, commissioned on June 30, 1497 and today housed in Milan, depicts Christ with his disciples on Passover before his crucifixion?

(1072) During his conquest of Italy, Napoleon stole and shipped renowned paintings and rare manuscripts back to France. From which library did he steal these works of art?

(1073) These ancient Roman structures of remarkably fine tolerances were built both aboveground and underground. One such structure, the Pont du Gard, descended only 17 meters in its entire 31 mile distance. Name this type of structure.

(1074) Legendary entertainer and conductor Guy Lombardo was born in 1902. In which country was he born? (Hint: not America, nor Italy)

(1075) Born in Pesaro on February 29, 1792, I am known for writing the musical score that became the best-known operatic music of all time as the theme to the television show *The Lone Ranger*. Who am I?

(1076) Born in Rimini on January 20, 1920, I am known for directing *La Strada* (1950) and *La Dolce Vita* (1960). Who am I?

(1077) Born in Vicenza in 1508, Andrea Palladio became a legend in his field and was one of the most imitated artists in the entire world. In which profession did he practice?

(1078) What country lends its name to the famous steps in Rome?

(1079) Name the Italian composer who won the Pulitzer Prize in 1957.

(1080) Which great Italian operatic composer, born on December 22, 1858 and known for dramatic realism of his operas, wrote *Madame Butterfly*, *Tosca* and *La Boheme*?

(1081) Born in Cremona in 1644, I am known by some as the greatest violin maker of all time with the most cherished violin label in the world. The Latin version of my name is inscribed on each instrument I produced. Who am I?

(1082) Born in Florence in 1377, I am known for completing what was considered near impossible work of designing and building the huge dome for Santa Maria del Fiore in Florence. Who am I?

(1083) Antonio Vivaldi, considered the greatest master of baroque music in the 18th century, produced how many total works (operas, sonatas, concertos) during his lifetime?

(1084) This French-born Italian designed the Statue of Liberty. Name him.

(1085) How many liters of water did aqueducts supply to ancient Rome each day?

(1086) After who was the face on the Statue of Liberty modeled?

(1087) Who is the first Italian woman to win a Grammy music award?

> ## IT HAPPENED IN...1743 A.D.
>
> ▶**Anna Maria Luisa**, last surviving member of the Medici family, dies in Florence. She bequeaths the substantial Medici family treasurers to the people for their benefit and for the curiosity of foreigners.

(1088) Beginning in the 1st century A.D., what special purpose did Domus Flavia and Domus Augustana hold?

(1089) Where did the first opera house open in 1637?

(1090) In which year did Arturo Toscanini make his debut at New York City's Metropolitan Opera House?

(1091) Although the Renaissance is purely Italian, the word Renaissance is not. In Italian, the word would be Rinascita or Renascimento. From which language do we get the word Renaissance?

(1092) This structure measured 48 meters high, 188 meters long, and 156 meters wide. There were 80 entrances - 76 for ordinary spectators, two for the imperial family and two for the gladiators. The first level of seating (or Podium) was for Roman senators and contained the emperor's private marble and cushioned box. Name this structure.

(1093) Some historians believe that the building of the Colosseum was financed by what activity?

(1094) When and where did opera originate?

(1095) The hymn, *Gesu Bambino*, written by Pietro A. Yon in 1919, is sung by Italians during which holiday season?

(1096) Amedeo Modigliani, the 20th century Italian artist born in Leghorn, Italy, was not Catholic. Of which religion was he?

(1097) Born Rodolpho Guglielmi in Castellaneta, Italy, this silent movie star was one of the first sex symbols of the big screen. By which name do we know him best?

(1098) Which renowned buildings in Russia were built and decorated by Italians on invitation from Emperor Peter the Great?

(1099) Some of the marble from the Roman Colosseum was used for the building of what world-renowned structure?

(1100) What is causing the Colosseum in Rome to slowly crumble?

(1101) What does the 1970 United Nations Educational, Scientific and Cultural Organization convention prohibit?

(1102) Who was the renowned 16th century architect from Vicenza, Italy that greatly influenced American colonial architecture?

(1103) The Renaissance, which literally means a rebirth or renewal, was an attempt to recapture the greatness of the ancient Romans and Greeks with respect to the arts, music and literature. When did the Renaissance occur?

(1104) Which famous Italian Renaissance artist was the illegitimate son of a Florentine notary and a peasant woman?

TOP 10 OF ITALY
Most Populated Provinces

	PROVINCE	POPULATION
1	Milan	3,869,037
2	Rome	3,831,959
3	Naples	3,086,622
4	Turin	2,242,775
5	Bari	1,595,359
6	Palermo	1,239,808
7	Brescia	1,182,337
8	Salerno	1,090,934
9	Catania	1,075,657
10	Bergamo	1,033,848

(1105) Which building, arguably the most renowned in all of Spain, was designed by Italian Pellegrino Tibaldi?

(1106) What event during the early 19th century inspired Tchaikovsky to compose *Capriccio Italian*?

(1107) In which year did construction begin on the 296 step Leaning Tower of Pisa?

(1108) Built by Appius Claudius in 312 B.C., this aqueduct was seven miles in length and ran primarily underground to protect against enemies and to minimize evaporation. Name this first aqueduct to serve ancient Rome.

(1109) Born in Parma on March 25, 1867, I am known as one of the greatest musical legends of the 20th century. Who am I?

(1110) AB-57 is a chemical compound used to clean and restore works in the Sistine Chapel. Whose work did they restore?

(1111) Operas *La Sonnambula* and *Norma* were written by which great Italian composer?

(1112) Who was the star of the 1961 Tony Award-winning Broadway play, *Carnival*?

(1113) What structure, built around 120 A.D., is considered the best-preserved building of ancient Rome?

(1114) Which Renaissance sculptor carved the Medici tombs of Florence?

(1115) Born in Florence in 1455, I am known for my famous paintings, *The Birth of Venus* and *The Adoration of the Magi*. Who am I?

(1116) According to some estimates, what percentage of all existing art in the world was created by Italians? (a) 22% (b) 33% (c) 60%

(1117) In what operatic role did Luciano Pavarotti make his singing debut when he filled in for a sick tenor?

(1118) What is the name of the famous sculpture inside Saint Peter's Basilica where Jesus is lying on his mother's knees?

(1119) Which northern Italian city is depicted in many of Canaletto's (1697 - 1768) paintings?

(1120) About how many ancient artifacts and priceless treasures are stolen each year from Italy and France combined and later sold for handsome profits?

(1121) *Six Characters in Search of an Author* is the most popular play of which Nobel Prize winning composer of Sicilian heritage?

(1122) *The Birth of Venus*, a painting by Sandro Botticelli, shows a nude woman rising from the sea in a large seashell. Who is the woman said to be depicted in this painting?

(1123) Which of Raphael's paintings is considered his most famous?

(1124) What does "prima donna" refer to in Italian?

(1125) Who wrote the lyrics for Giuseppe Verdi's opera, *Il Trovatore*?

(1126) Born in Venice on March 4, 1678, I am known as one of the greatest composers of all time. During my lifetime, I composed over 800 authenticated musical works. Many consider *Four Seasons* to be my greatest work. Who am I?

(1127) The exterior of the Cathedral of Maria del Fiore in Florence is comprised of three types of marble - each type presenting a different color. Name the three colors.

(1128) What is the Italian name for a female ballet dancer?

(1129) How did the La Scala opera house in Milan get its name?

(1130) Which bandleader made a name for himself performing on New Year's Eve telecasts from Manhattan?

(1131) Where and when was the tenor Mario Del Monaco born?

(1132) Which 16th century Italian composer, a popular religious composer, wrote over 100 mass and other religious compositions?

(1133) What was the name of the Roman theater where the opera *Tosca*, a story set in Rome during political division between the Bonapartists and the Monarchists, was first produced?

(1134) Which Italian journalist wrote the classic book, *The Italians*?

(1135) What honor does the 1930 motion picture, *La Canzone dell'Amore*, hold?

(1136) William Shakespeare used Italian settings for many of his plays. How many travels to Italy did he make?

(1137) Born in Castelfranco Veneto in 1477, I am known for my famous painting, *The Tempest*. Who am I?

(1138) How many awards (Grammy, Emmy, Academy) did composer Enrico Mancini win?

(1139) What occurs during an intermezzo?

(1140) In which century was the violin virtuoso, Nicola Paganini, born?

(1141) What is the name of Europe's largest film studio complex, referred to as "Hollywood on the Tiber"?

(1142) Which Italian opera star was born in Bari in 1913?

(1143) Tiziano is considered the greatest Renaissance painter of which city?

(1144) This type of musical production is similar to an opera, but with religious connotations and without background scenery. What is the name of this production?

(1145) Michelangelo's last work, albeit unfinished, can be found in the Castello Sforzecso. Name this work.

(1146) Name the great Italian opera tenor that was the very first to sell over one million music albums.

(1147) Which Walt Disney movie used the backdrop from Amilcare Ponchielli's musical masterpiece, *Dance of the Hours*?

(1148) Michelangelo did not inscribe his name on any of the works he produced, except for one, *La Pieta*. Why?

(1149) Which Italian word, now part of the English language, refers to singing without the use of music or background sounds?

(1150) The *Golden Apple* was an opera written in honor of the 1667 marriage of Emperor Leopold I and performed in Vienna. Which Italian is thus credited with introducing opera to Vienna?

(1151) During Christmas, Italian bagpipes are typically played by shepherds. What is the name of this instrument?

(1152) How long did Leonardo da Vinci take to paint the *Mona Lisa*?

(1153) Where can you find a replica of the statue of *David*?

(1154) This literary great was the first to write a major literary work in the vernacular rather than in Latin. He is also considered the father of the Italian language. Name him.

(1155) Born in Cremona in 1567, I am known as the father of the modern opera and wrote the first opera, *Orfeo*. Who am I?

(1156) Which great present-day Italian tenor holds a Doctorate of Law from the University of Pisa? (Hint: sang at the closing ceremony of the 2006 Olympic games in Turin)

(1157) Born in 1240, I am known as the Italian painter who bridged the gap between Byzantine art of the Middle Ages and Renaissance art. Who am I?

(1158) What exquisite international art gallery houses the famed *Mona Lisa* painting by Da Vinci?

(1159) Born in Lajatico in rural Tuscany on September 22, 1958, I am presently one of the greatest tenors in the world. I began my signing career in 1993 and unfortunately lost my sight completely at the age of 12 after being hit in the head by a soccer ball. Who am I?

(1160) What terrestrial phenomenon can be seen in the upper portion of *The Adoration of the Magi* by the great Italian painter Giotto?

IT HAPPENED IN...1654 A.D.

► **Queen Christina of Sweden, a convert to Catholicism, abdicates her throne and immigrates to Rome where she takes up residence. There she will commission many paintings and musical productions. She is buried at the Vatican.**

(1161) Name the most treasured opera from composer Vincenzo Bellini.

(1162) What is Michelangelo's last name?

(1163) The harpsichord was invented in Italy during the 15th century. In which city was the harpsichord invented including its center of production?

(1164) What is used to create the colored paint used in a fresco?

(1165) This series of films, starring Clint Eastwood and set in the American west during the 19th century, was actually filmed in Italy during the 1960s. Name this film series.

(1166) Born in Vespignano in 1267, I am remembered as the person who best defined modern Western art. Most people know me by my first name only. Who am I?

(1167) Which Italian pioneer was considered the greatest realism painter of the Renaissance? (a) Giotto (b) Botticelli (c) Masaccio

(1168) The Renaissance began in what part of Italy? (a) southern (b) central (c) northern

(1169) Rome has two of the oldest public museums in the world. One contains Roman and Greek sculptures and the other contains sculptures, frescoes and artwork. Name these two museums.

(1170) Who was the most popular person painted during the Renaissance?

(1171) To replace the harpsichord, an instrument that produced sounds too low for large concert halls, Italian Andrea Amati (1505-1574) invented which monumental string instrument during the late Renaissance?

(1172) What Italian word refers to the best musicians and conductors?

(1173) Which Italian film director introduced the "Spaghetti Western"?

(1174) Born in Urbino on April 6, 1483, I am considered the central painter of the High Renaissance and studied under Leonardo da Vinci and Michelangelo. Unfortunately, I died at the early age of 37. Who am I?

(1175) Mozart's opera, *Cosi Fan Tutte*, is set in which Italian city during the 18th century?

(1176) Who is considered the "Father of the Violin"? (Hint: from Salo, Italy)

(1177) What instrument, invented by Roman architect Vitruvius in the 1st century B.C., was Italian musician and harpsichord conductor Domenico Scarlatti most famous?

(1178) The Camerata, or Camerata dei Bardi, was a group of Italian musicians. What was their goal?

(1179) Name two of Enrico Mancini's hit musical scores.

(1180) Which two prominent American historical buildings closely resemble the well-preserved Roman temple of Maison Carree, located in Nimes, France?

(1181) Antonello da Messina introduced what form of painting to Italy during the early Renaissance?

(1182) The famous Castel of Sant' Angelo was originally built as a mausoleum to which Emperor? (Hint: he also built a wall in present-day England)

(1183) Where does the majority of the setting of *Madame Butterfly* take place?

(1184) What type of foundation is used for a fresco, a term meaning fresh in Italian?

(1185) Born Salvatore Guaragna in Brooklyn in 1893, this Italian American is remembered for composing songs *Chattanooga Choo-Choo* and *An Affair to Remember*. By what name do we remember him best?

(1186) This imposing French structure, commissioned in 1806 by Napoleon, was styled after triumphal arches invented and built throughout Europe by the Romans. Name this structure located in Paris.

(1187) This great opera, based on William Shakespeare's *Merry Wives of Windsor* and *King Henry IV*, is Giuseppe Verdi's last opera. Name this opera.

(1188) This form of music and production was invented in Florence in the late 16th to early 17th century with the release of *Orfeo*, written by Claudio Monteverdi, in 1607. Name this form of music.

(1189) Born in Florence on March 6, 1475, I am known for painting the frescoes on the ceiling of the Sistine Chapel. Who am I?

(1190) The Pantheon, considered the best-preserved building of ancient Rome, was constructed by Emperor Hadrian around 120 A.D. and incorporated a hemispherical dome set upon a rotunda. Originally dedicated as the "Temple for All the Gods", for whom was the Pantheon rededicated when Christianity became the official religion of the Roman Empire?

(1191) Born near Venice around 1488, this master painter of the Italian Renaissance is considered one of the world's greatest master colorists. He is also considered the last great artist of the Renaissance. Name him.

(1192) Which great Italian writer wrote *De Monarchia*?

(1193) Where was the longest ancient Roman aqueduct located? (Hint: not in Italy)

(1194) *La Gioconda* is the alternate title for the *Mona Lisa*. Name the great Renaissance artist who produced this painting, considered the most famous and single most recognizable painting in the entire world.

(1195) Which church in Florence is considered one of Italy's most perfect examples of Gothic architecture?

(1196) Name the opera considered to have the oldest known musical score.

(1197) Parco della Musica (Music Park) is the largest concert hall and open-air arena in all of Europe. This complex cost $140 million to build. Where is the Parco della Musica located?

(1198) How does famous Italian tenor Luciano Pavarotti refer to his singing voice?

(1199) Which Roman emperor authorized the building of the ancient Roman Colosseum, begun in 79 A.D.?

(1200) What is the name of the great opera house in Rome, built in 1880?

(1201) Who was the composer of *Stairway to the Stars*, *Blue Serenade* and *I'll Never Be the Same*?

(1202) Who wrote the opera *Triumph of Saint Joan*?

(1203) In which region of Italy has the marionette theater experienced its greatest popularity?

(1204) The movie, *La Dolce Vita*, introduced to the world which word that describes pushy and aggressive photographers?

(1205) Who composed the popular song *Avalon*?

(1206) Where can you visit Michelangelo's tomb?

CHAPTER
E·L·E·V·E·N
XI

SCIENCES, BIOLOGY, & INVENTION

Contributions Italians Have Given to the World

"A great flame follows a little spark."

- DANTE ALIGHIERI

"It is no good to try to stop knowledge from going forward. Ignorance is never better than knowledge."

- ENRICO FERMI

(1207) Enrico Bombieri received the highly prestigious Fields Medal in 1974 for his work in what scientific field? (Hint: there is no Noble Prize in this field, thus the Fields Medal is the top award internationally)

(1208) At which university did Galileo Galilei teach? (a) Pisa (b) Bologna (c) Padua

(1209) Dr. Santoria, a 17th century Italian physician, is credited with inventing what device to measure human temperature?

(1210) Born in Modena in 1523, I am known for discovering the narrow ducts in the female reproductive system that bears my name. Who am I?

(1211) Which Italian scientist is credited with discovering the concept of energy?

IT HAPPENED IN...1978 A.D.

► **Polish Cardinal Karol Wojtyla, archbishop of Cracow, is elected pope, the first non-Italian pope in over 400 years. Wojtyla takes the name of John Paul II.**

(1212) What distinction does the Parco Nazionale del Gran Paradiso, opened in 1821 and located in Aosta Valley (Valle d'Aosta), hold?

(1213) To protect both creditors and labors, what type of property claim was introduced in Italy around the 15th century?

(1214) From which region do many florists in Italy obtain their flowers?

(1215) Mathematician Gregorio Ricci (1853 - 1925) was the leading developer of a form of mathematics that is not only the foundation for Tensor Calculus, but also is the basis for Albert Einstein's theory of relativity. What form of mathematics did this Italian develop?

(1216) Born in Lombardy on July 7, 1843, I won the Nobel Prize for medicine in 1906 for my discovery and research of nerve fiber ends, which now bear my name. Who am I?

(1217) What type of fencing was invented by an Italian?

(1218) In America, the voltage of electrical outlets is 120. What is the voltage in Italy and the rest of Europe?

(1219) Leonardo Fibonacci introduced which mathematical symbol, employed extensively today, to the world in the 13th century?

(1220) Antonio Stradivari introduced a unique design element for violins that rewrote musical history. Guitars, violas and cellos use his invention as well. What did he invent?

(1221) In 1801, Giuseppe Piazzi, astronomer and director of the Palermo Observatory, made what major discovery?

(1222) Born in Genoa on October 10, 1946, Franco Egidio Malerba, Ph.D. is an Italian astronaut and member of the European Parliament (MEP). What honor of distinction does he hold?

(1223) According to scientific research, Italian men are 90% less likely than American men to die from what cause?

(1224) This Italian archeologist, born in Padua, discovered eight ancient Egyptian tombs in the Valley of the Kings, including that of Seti I discovered in 1817. He is also credited with being the first person of the modern age to discover the openings and enter both Abu Simbel and the Great Pyramid of Khafre. Name this archeologist.

(1225) Angelo Barovier is credited with perfecting a type of glass that is highly prized throughout the world. Name this type of glass.

(1226) Born in Bologna on April 25, 1874 to an Italian father and Irish mother (herself an heir to the Jamison whiskey fortune), I am known for inventing the wireless radio. When I died in 1937, every radio station in the world observed two minutes of silence in my honor. President Howard William Taft even called me the "world's greatest benefactor". Who am I?

(1227) What was the name of the seaplane that transmitted the first message via radio to a ground station in 1928?

(1228) This dance was invented by Italians in the courts of Florence during the late 15th century. Italians named this dance the ballare, which means to dance. However, the French word for ballare was adopted since the first books and first school for this dance were introduced in France. Name this dance.

(1229) Girolamo Cardano was the first person to solve difficult cubic mathematical equations. For this and his pioneering work in statistics, specifically objectively researching dice rolling and other games of chance, he is known as the father of what science?

(1230) The first medical school in the Western world was established in the 9th century in which Italian city?

(1231) To protect soldiers from the elements of weather - specifically their feet, ankles, and neck - what articles of clothing did the ancient Romans introduce to the world?

(1232) Resveratrol, an anti-oxidant found in wine, is said to help slow what biological process?

(1233) In 1900, Enrico Forlanini invented the first true mechanism that lifted and propelled boats. Later versions enabled boats to reach speeds of 50 miles per hour. What did he invent?

(1234) Established in the 11th century, this university was the first university in all of Europe. Name this renowned university.

(1235) An Italian café owner is credited with introducing the first ice cream. In which European city was the first ice cream introduced and sold?

(1236) This type of instruction book was introduced in the early 17th century by Agostini Agazzari. What type of instruction did this book provide?

(1237) This game, originally called quotis, was invented in Rome using flattened iron rings. The rings were tossed at two different stakes located 18 feet apart and 1 inch from the ground. Name this outdoor game invented by Italians.

(1238) According to Roman mythology, the goddess of flowers is synonymous with flowers and vegetation from a particular area. Name this goddess of mythology.

(1239) What element of design did the ancient Romans incorporate into shoes around 200 B.C.?

(1240) Italians Vincenzo Viviani and Giovanni Alfonso Borelli were the first to accurately measure what type of speed in the 17th century? (Hint: they estimated the speed at 1,148 feet per second)

(1241) In 1890, Italian Giuseppe Airoldi invented a language thinking puzzle that today can be found in most newspapers across the globe. What puzzle did he invent?

TOP 10 OF ITALY
Largest Lakes

	LAKE	AREA	LOCATION
1	Garda	370	Lombardy, Trentino-Alto Adige, Veneto
2	Maggiore	212	Lombardy & Piedmont
3	Como	146	Lombardy
4	Trasimeno	128	Umbria
5	Bolsena	115	Lazio
6	Iseo	65	Lombardy
7	Varano	61	Apulia
8	Bracciano	58	Lazio
9	Lesina	52	Apulia
10	Lugano	51	Lombardy

Area is in Square Kilometers

(1242) Born in Rome on September 29, 1901, I am known for my groundbreaking work with atomic particles that lead to the development of the atomic bomb. In 1938, I received the Nobel Prize for this work. Who am I?

(1243) Venetians are known for their skill in crafting glass. What unique type of glass did they introduce that made looking through glass much easier?

(1244) Which musical instrument did Italians invent that is based on the violin?

(1245)   What type of glassware did the ancient Romans introduce around 50 B.C.?

(1246)   In Latin, "caeso matris utere" is a birth by Caesarian section. Which Roman general, perhaps the most famous of all generals, was born this way?

(1247)   What article of clothing did Italians invent that originated from the Italian comic character, Saint Pantaleone?

(1248)   In 1920, Italian Guglielmo Marconi established the first public broadcasting radio station in the United Kingdom. This station was the precursor of which leading international radio network broadcast from Britain?

IT HAPPENED IN...1959 A.D.

▶ The Second Vatican Council is held at the summons of Pope John XXIII. The aim of the council is to review and enact reforms in the Church to renew spiritual life.

(1249)   For what reason does Italy have scarce mineral deposits and fossil fuels?

(1250)   What unique technique are some wine makers in Italy using to protect against others counterfeiting their wines, thus protecting the authenticity?

(1251)   Domenico Bandini is credited with compiling and introducing a modern series of books in the 15th century that became the leading source of reference information. Name this series of books that has recently been replaced by the Internet.

(1252)   This person invented, constructed, and used the first microscopes, lens, and telescopes. In using the telescope, he became the first person to view the rings of Saturn in 1610. Name this person.

(1253)   An Italian company was recently awarded the job of restoring part of a wonder of the ancient world. This wonder runs for nearly 4,000 miles and is recognizable from space. Name this wonder of the ancient world.

(1254) The first public hospital was established by the Romans in 372 A.D. in the province of Caesarea. In which city was the second hospital established? (a) Rome (b) Byzantium (c) Carthage (d) Athens

(1255) In the late 15th century, Cosimo de' Medici established the famous Ospedale Degli Innocenti in Florence. What civilization "first" did he thus establish?

(1256) The survivors of the 1912 Titanic sinking presented a golden plaque to Guglielmo Marconi in recognition of his instrumental role in their rescue. Why was he given this recognition?

(1257) Which major city in Italy has one of the highest recorded levels of sulfur dioxide pollution in the world?

(1258) What did astronomer Giovanni Schiaparelli, director of the Brera Observatory in Milan, discover?

(1259) Guido d'Arezzo, an 11th century Italian Benedictine monk and choir master of a Benedictine monastery, introduced the assignment of syllables to musical notations (A through G) to represent pitch. Which assignment did he introduce that revolutionized music forever?

(1260) Italian American Bernard Cousino patented a type of music tape player, only to be rendered obsolete shortly thereafter by the cassette player. Name his invention.

(1261) Filippo Cecchi, a 19th century Catholic priest, invented a scientific instrument that monitors, measures, and records vibrations in the subsurface of the Earth. What did he invent?

(1262) Where in Italy would you see a "green cross ambulance"?

(1263) The ancient Romans invented this device around 400 B.C. to shield their villas from the outside weather. However, only the provinces in northern Europe typically employed this invention. What did the Romans invent?

(1264) Combining barium sulfate and powdered coal, Italian cobbler and alchemist Vincenzo Cascariolo invented what mixture?

(1265) Galileo was said to have tested his theories of mass, weight and gravity from the top of the Leaning Tower of Pisa. Is this claim fact or fiction?

(1266) What musical form, developed by Pope Saint Gregory I in the 6th century, is considered the beginning of Western music?

(1267) Although numbered playing cards were developed in China, what unique element did Italians add to playing cards in the early 14th century?

(1268) During the Renaissance, Italians invented which article of cloth typically used when people sneeze?

(1269) For what invention did Guglielmo Marconi win the Nobel Prize for physics in 1909?

(1270) In America, the number to dial in emergency situations is 911. What do you dial when in Italy for the same reason?

(1271) This activity, considered both a game and a method of making decisions, was introduced by the ancient Romans - most notably Julius Caesar. Referred to as "caput aut navis" (ship or chief) by the Romans, this activity was widely used for civil and criminal disputes. Name this activity. (Hint: used before football games)

(1272) While employed by the United States Army Air Force, Gino Santi invented a life-saving device in 1947 that today is found in all fighter jets throughout the world. Name this device.

(1273) What common building material did the ancient Romans invent and use extensively for the construction of mighty buildings, bridges, and aqueducts?

(1274) Which Italian words are used to mark the speed or tempo of musical compositions indicated by a series of directions?

(1275) During the 13th century, Florentine Salvino Armati, with the help of Alessandro della Spina, a Dominican monk, invented a type of glass lens that assisted in correcting vision. Name this invention.

(1276) Mathematician Niccolo Tartaglia solved what degree of equation? (a) second (b) third (c) fourth (d) fifth

(1277) To escape persecution of the Jews, this atomic physicist fled Italy in 1938 and immigrated to America. That same year he won the Noble Prize for physics. Name him.

(1278) The Latin abbreviation A.D. (as in the year 2006 A.D.) is short for Anno Domini. What does Anno Domini mean in English?

(1279) To which city in Italy did sailors from Genoa bring back the Black Death plague to Europe from China via the Crimea (present-day Ukraine) in A.D. 1347?

(1280) Carrying on the Venetian tradition of glassblowing, Italian Carlo Riva invented and manufactured the first type of this glass in Venice in 1713. What type of glass did he invent? (Hint: think of the hull of boats)

(1281) What was the distance of an ancient Roman mile?

TOP 10 OF ITALY

Least Populated Provinces

	PROVINCE	POPULATION
1	Isernia	89,577
2	Aosta	123,978
3	Gorizia	141,196
4	Oristano	153,935
5	Rieti	154,406
6	Verb-Cus-Ossola	161,580
7	Vibo Valentia	168,481
8	Crotone	172,374
9	Enna	174,199
10	Vercelli	177,027

(1282) When and by whom was the Oboe, a modern-day musical instrument, invented?

(1283) Although the Romans (under Julius Caesar) are credited with inventing a crude version of a newspaper in 59 B.C., the first modern newspaper was published in Italy in 1563. Name the city.

(1284) The first formal academy of the arts was founded in the mid-16th century in which Italian city?

(1285) Which absolutely essential mathematical symbol was introduced in Italy during the 15th century?

(1286) This city, the second largest in southern Italy, was devastated by the Black Death plague that killed nearly 80% of its inhabitants. Name this city.

(1287) This Italian Renaissance scientist introduced the first solution for measuring longitude using the moons of Jupiter as a way to accurately set a clock, a crucial factor in measuring longitude. Name this scientist.

(1288) During the 1st century, ancient Romans invented what type of heating system they called hypocaust?

(1289) This ancient Roman invention consisted of a cylinder into which water dripped from a reservoir allowing water levels to be measured against a scale. Invented in the 2nd century B.C., this early instrument of measurement was called the clepsydra. What was its purpose?

(1290) Galileo Galilei was forced to reject his belief that the earth moves around the sun and instead publicly state that the earth is the center of the galaxy. What famous words did he utter under his breath before he died?

(1291) Italian Guido d'Arezzo made possible the transcription of musical notes to a four-line graph, thus revolutionizing musical composition. Name his invention.

(1292) Which musical instrument was developed in Italy during the mid-19th century?

(1293) Born in Turin in 1912, this Italian immigrated to the United States in 1940 and became a U.S. citizen in 1947. He was awarded the Nobel Prize in 1969 for his research which proved that viruses undergo permanent changes and spontaneously create mutant strains. He was honored for helping to "set the solid foundation on which modern molecular biology rest". Name him.

(1294) What nursery rhyme, sung even today by young children, was inspired by the catastrophic Black Death plague?

(1295) The ancient Romans were the first to build this type of structure in northern Europe and built them extensively in the eastern Mediterranean. This structure was built at Dover, England and Boulogna, France to aid in the crossing of the English Channel. Name this type of structure.

(1296) During the 1st century, the ancient Romans were the first people to use this fire burning illumination instrument. Name this invention typically made of vegetable and animal fats during the Roman era.

(1297) What did the ancient Romans invent to aid them on their journeys to distant and foreign lands?

(1298) Born in Como on February 18, 1745, I am known for my work with electricity and for building the first battery in the year 1800. For this work I am considered the founder of electrochemistry. Who am I?

(1299) Italy is credited with introducing a type of satirical cartoon in the 17th century that is found in nearly every newspaper today. Name this type of cartoon.

(1300) The ancient Romans invented "pouzzolana cement" for the construction of bridges and sewers. What was so special about pouzzolana cement?

(1301) Strong evidence, including a patent, supports the claim that Italian Antonio Meucci invented this communication device in 1871, twenty years before Alexander Graham Bell claimed to have invented it. Name this communication device.

(1302) Legendary Greek philosopher Aristotle claimed that heavier bodies fall faster than lighter bodies fall. Which Italian Renaissance scientist proved Aristotle's claim false?

(1303) What is the name given to the gruesome plague that ravaged Italy and Europe during the late Middle Ages and what percentage of the Italian population did it eradicate?

(1304) Carlo Rubbia won the Nobel Prize in 1984 for his discovery that provided proof of the weak-force theory of physics. What did he discover?

(1305) In the 16th century, Florentine Vincenzo Peruzzi was the first to cut this stone, today one of the most valuable in the world. What stone did Peruzzi cut to create brilliants?

(1306) Where can you find on display the lectern Galileo Galilei used when he taught physics as a professor?

(1307) What did Vincenzo Lanciais, an automotive engineer, invent?

(1308) In 1571, the first public library in the world opened in Italy. Name the city where this library was located.

(1309) The first two botanical gardens in the world were established in 1543 and 1545 in Italy by Cosimo de' Medici. Name the Italian city in which both were established.

(1310) What type of travel aid, providing direction and distance to Rome, was invented and used extensively by the ancient Romans?

(1311) In an effort to control the volume of the harpsichord, Italian inventor Bartolommeo Cristofori invented the modern piano. Cristofori originally called his piano "gravicembalo con piano e forte". What does this name mean in English?

(1312) This form of secret code was first developed and employed by the ancient Romans to render their messages undecipherable to the enemy. This form involved substitution and was commonly referred to as the Julius Caesar method. What did the Romans invent?

(1313) Stradivarius violins are considered the finest violins in the world. The U.S. Library of Congress has a Stradivari Memorial where five Stradivarius violins are housed in a temperature-controlled showcase. Name the specific make of Stradivarius violin that is considered the undisputed king of violins.

(1314) In which Italian city was the modern wedding ring introduced around the 15th century?

(1315) In 1910, Italian radio inventor, Guglielmo Marconi, successfully sent radio messages from Ireland to a South American country over 6,000 miles away. Name this country.

(1316) The origin of denim jeans can be traced to 15th century Italy. However, the term "jeans" was coined by the French. In which coastal city where denim jeans invented?

(1317) Cloaca Maxima was a network of engineered tunnels under ancient Rome. What specifically was the Cloaca Maxima?

(1318) The ancient Romans were the first to introduce this musical element using the first 15 letters of the alphabet as notes. Name this element of musical inscription.

(1319) Archimedes, an ancient Greek mathematician born on the island of Sicily and killed at the battle of Syracuse in 212 B.C. by invading Roman legions, invented what mathematical term that revolutionized geometry forever?

(1320) Who is most often cited as the first Renaissance painter and father of modern art? (Hint: a Florentine known by his first name)

(1321) Although refined centuries later, what scientific contribution for measuring time in days, weeks, and months did Julius Caesar give to the world?

(1322) People from which Italian city claim to have invented the table napkin and the fork?

(1323) Italians introduced a now common type of insurance that financially protects people against pre-mature death. Name this type of insurance.

(1324) The very first ordinance requiring street lighting was established in Italy during the 12th century. Name the city.

(1325) What number does the Roman numeral CD represent?

(1326) This type of field hospital was invented by the ancient Romans. Archaeologists have found scalpels, clamps, sutures and other necessary medical emergency items at historic battlefields. What is the generic name for this type of hospital invented by the ancient Romans?

(1327) Alcohol was first distilled at this school during the Middle Ages. Name this school that introduced alcohol to the world.

(1328) Born in Pisa in 1180, I am known for introducing Arabic numerals, which quickly replaced the archaic Roman numeral system, to Italy and the rest of Europe. Who am I?

(1329) What type of organization was developed in Renaissance Italy to protect trade and commerce?

(1330) The world's first boat race was held in Italy in 1300. In which city was this event held?

(1331) What modern-day office machine did Giuseppe Ravizza invent in the 19th century?

(1332) Which two months of the present-day calendar are named after ancient Roman emperors?

IT HAPPENED IN...1945 A.D.

▶Mussolini attempts to escape into neutral Switzerland disguised as a German soldier. He and his mistress are captured near Lake Como by Italian partisans and brought to Azzano. There the two are shot dead by partisan colonel Walter Audisio. Their bodies are brought to Milan and hung upside-down in Piazzale Loreto.

(1333) Considered the father of ballistic science, this Italian mathematician wrote the first book about applying mathematics to artillery firing and published the first firing tables. Name this 16th century Italian.

(1334) What is the name for the giant missile launcher, a weapon used extensively during sieges, the ancient Romans invented? (Hint: the word ballistics originated from this weapon)

(1335) The Borsa family, bankers from Venice, established the first stock exchange in the world in the late 14th century in the town of Bruges. Shortly after arriving, the Borsas changed their name to der Bourse. In which European country did they open this stock exchange?

(1336) Michelangelo's famous *David* statue, housed in the Galleria dell'Accademia, is located in which Italian city?

(1337) Italian physicist Giovanni Caselli invented the pantelegraph, considered the first working telegraph for graphics, and placed this machine in operation between Paris and Marseille in 1856. What early communication machine did he invent?

(1338) Post office boxes were first introduced in Italy in 1820. Name the town where they were first introduced.

(1339) This family from Pomone, Italy, is credited with inventing the toothpick propeller used during World War I by the Allied nations. However, their most famous invention was the whirlpool bath and hot tub. Name this family of seven brothers.

(1340) At its height of power, ancient Rome was supplied with water from eleven aqueducts. What was their combined distance in miles?

(1341) What color was invented in a northern Italian town, once an important silk town, which bears its name?

(1342) Alessandro Volta, an Italian professor of physics at the University of Pavia, invented an important electrical device made of zinc and copper plates. So impressed was French leader Napoleon Bonaparte that he bestowed the title of Count on Volta. What did he invent?

CHAPTER 11

(1343) What early safe-sex product did Gabriel Fallopius, an anatomy professor at the University of Padua, invent during the 16th century?

(1344) Who were the Medici Condotti?

(1345) What type of fragrance did Italian John Maria Farura invent during the 18th century while living in Cologne, Germany?

(1346) Famous Italian mathematician, Girolamo Cardano, is credited with inventing the original concept for what language in the 16th century? (Hint: uses a combination of symbols and signs)

(1347) This Italian physicist theorized that solid bodies fall at speeds independent of their mass, after discounting the resistance of air. This work was documented in the 1638 book, *In Discourses and Mathematical Demonstrations Concerning Two New Sciences*. Name this Italian physicist.

(1348) Born in Faenza on October 15, 1608, I am known for my invention of the barometer, an instrument that greatly enhanced weather forecasts. I was also the first person to sustain a manmade vacuum. Who am I?

(1349) Which highly explosive and unstable chemical compound did chemist Ascanio Sobrero discover in 1847 at the University of Torino?

(1350) Carlo Collodi, born Carlo Lorenzini, was the creator of a famous fairytale character that could not hide his lies. Name the character he created.

(1351) What form of legal protection covering intellectual property was first granted in Florence during the 15th century?

(1352) Leonardo da Vinci never published his written notes. What else is surprising and unique about the way he produced his written notes?

(1353) In 1895, Italian Giuseppe Peano first used this Greek letter to signify the sum of numbers. Identify this commonly used symbol of mathematical set theory.

(1354) What medical instrument was invented by Italian Gattinara in the 15th century that allowed for fluid injection and retrieval from the human body?

(1355) Born in Padua on May 4, 1655, I was an inventor of musical instruments for Ferdinando de' Medici, the Grand Prince of Tuscany. History remembers me for inventing the modern piano in Florence in 1709. Who am I?

(1356) Italian Flavio Gioia of Campania is credited with inventing what device for measuring geographic direction?

(1357) The forerunner of the modern-day carjack, parachute, and bicycle were designed by which great Italian Renaissance man?

(1358) Which two Italians invented the internal-combustion engine in 1852?

CHAPTER
T·W·E·L·V·E
XII

SPORTS, LEISURE, & FASHION

Italian Entertainment, Pastime, and Lifestyle

❝*When somebody screws up in front of you at 200 miles per hour, man, school's out.***❞**

- MARIO ANDRETTI

❝*When baseball is no longer fun it's no longer a game.***❞**

- JOE DIMAGGIO

(1359) Previous to the 2006 World Cup championship, Italy was champion in 1982 when they beat West Germany 3-1. How many times has Italy won the men's soccer world championship?

(1360) How many points are needed for a victory in Bocce?

(1361) Who wrote the epic poem *Orlando Furioso* in the 16th century?

(1362) What dark period in Italian and European history began after the fall of the Roman Empire and lasted until the Renaissance?

(1363) Name the classic silent movie of 1922 in which Italian sex symbol Rudolph Valentino plays the role of a Spanish bullfighter?

(1364) How many animals were said to have died in the one hundred days of celebration which inaugurated the opening of the ancient Roman Colosseum?

(1365) What is the name of the popular Italian game which is similar to bowling?

(1366) What historical boat race takes place on the Grand Canal in Venice?

(1367) The English term "garb" derives it roots from which Italian word?

(1368) Introduced by the Etruscans, chariot races were very popular with the ancient Romans. What is the term they used to describe the area where chariot races were held?

(1369) Born in Italy, this legendary racecar driver is the only person to win the Formula One world championship, the Daytona 500 and the Indy 500. Name this racecar driver that immigrated to the United States.

(1370) When in public, Roman citizens typically wore what type of outer garment?

(1371) Born in Roncole on October 7, 1813, I am known as one of the greatest composers of all time. My first opera was *Oberto* and my most famous opera was *La Traviata* (*The Wayward Woman*). Who am I?

(1372) Born in Rome on September 20, 1934, I am an actor who received an Academy Award in 1961 for the movie *Two Women*. This award marked the first time in history that a female actor in a non-English speaking role was selected. Who am I?

(1373) Some evidence points to soccer originating in Italy during the 15th century. Under what name was this early version of soccer called?

(1374) What is a "mastrucca"?

(1375) Name the woman tennis player of Italian heritage who became the youngest Wimbledon semi-finalist since 1887.

> # IT HAPPENED IN...1936 A.D.
>
> ▶ **The Spanish Civil War rages between the Nationalist forces, commanded by General Francisco Franco, and the Republican government. To aid and support Franco, Mussolini sends 70,000 Italian soldiers to Spain.**

(1376) What is the name of the Sardinian article of clothing that resembles the Scottish kilt?

(1377) In which year did Italy win the coveted Davis Cup? (a) 1968 (b) 1976 (c) 1982 (d) 1994

(1378) What is the name of the 1981 movie in which Luciano Pavarotti appeared?

(1379) Which team sport is the second most popular in Italy?

(1380) Which Italian athlete is the first outside Scandinavia or the former Soviet Union to win the 50km cross-country event at the Olympics?

(1381) This man, the son of a leather craftsman from Florence, gained an appreciation for style and clothing during his travels to Paris and London. He opened his first store in 1920 in Florence and his clothing and goods quickly became the rage. Name this designer. (Hint: a popular purse line)

(1382) What is Sofia Loren's birth name?

(1383) Sophia Loren's sister was once married to the son of which famous and notorious Italian dictator?

(1384) Which Italian city is considered the capital of Italian fashion and style?

(1385) Name the European country from which the card game of briscola was introduced to Italy in the 16th century.

(1386) In Italy, if you see a hotel sign saying "al bergo divrno", what type of service does this hotel offer?

(1387) The famous designer, Giorgio Armani, pursued a career in what field early in his life?

(1388) From where did Sotirio Bulgari, the founder of Bulgari jewelry, emigrate before arriving in Italy with just $0.18 to his name?

(1389) The term "pensione" is no longer officially used in Italy to describe a hotel accommodation. However, the term can be found in remote locations. What is your specific accommodation if you are staying at a pensione?

(1390) Which leading Italian fashion designer designed the modern uniforms of the Italian police force?

(1391) Which modern sport originated from Italian bocce?

(1392) Born in Brooklyn on July 18, 1940, I won the Golden Glove award in 1965 and was named to nine All-Star games. Today, I manage the New York Yankees. Who am I?

(1393) What form of gambling, most likely introduced in Venice, was established as a state run lottery in the early 16th century?

(1394) During the ancient Roman era, this type of structure referred to a villa farm-house estate that was permanently occupied by servants, but typically only seasonally occupied by the owner. Name this type of structure.

(1395) Approximately how much was spent by Italy on the 2006 Winter Olympics in Turin?

(1396) What trophy, named for an Italian American, is given to the winner of the NFL's SuperBowl?

(1397) What is the most popular sport in Italy?

(1398) Italian Canadian brothers, Phil "Mr. Clutch" Esposito and Tony Esposito, were offensive and defensive powerhouses in this sport. They earned numerous trophies and awards, including the leagues most valuable player. In what cool sport did they play?

(1399) Who was called the "prince of fashion", but was sadly gunned down in 1997 outside his South Beach, Florida home?

(1400) Which monster film series did Italian American producer, Albert Broccoli, produce?

(1401) This Italian soccer player won the Golden Ball trophy for the 1993-1994 season, thus recognizing him as Europe's top soccer player. Name him.

1922 A.D. ▶ Mussolini becomes prime minister after "March on Rome"

(1402) Which Italian actress, born in 1859, was considered by most critics of her time as the greatest Italian actress of the early silent screen?

(1403) When did modern Italy legalize divorce?

(1404) How many spectators could the Roman Colosseum accommodate at one time?

(1405) Where was Mario Andretti, a famous race car driver from Italy, born on February 28, 1940?

(1406) A millinery shop is a hat shop. From which Italian city did this shop originate?

CHAPTER
T·H·I·R·T·E·E·N

TRAVEL, DESTINATIONS, & GEOGRAPHY

Revealing Italian Hotspots and Spectacular Locations

❝*Now, at last, I have arrived in the first city of the world!*❞

**- GERMAN POET JOHANN WOLFGANG VON GOETHE,
UPON ARRIVING IN ROME IN 1786**

❝*The goal I seek is to have people refine their style through my clothing without having them become victims of fashion.*❞

- GIORGIO ARMANI

(1407) What is the only region in Italy that does not have two or more provinces?

(1408) This town was founded by Frederick II in 1240 and features a 99-headed fountain built in 1272. Name this town.

(1409) What distinction does the Italian town of Casere hold?

(1410) This town was the first Greek colony in Italy. Today, only ruins remain as this town was razed to the ground by the Arabs in the 9th century. Name this town.

(1411) What was added to the Leaning Tower of Pisa in 1994 to shore up the tower and keep it from additional leaning?

(1412) The Palazzo Pitti, began in 1457 A.D. for the banker Luca Pitti, became the main residence of this influential Florentine family and now houses their treasures. Name this former leading family of Florence.

(1413) In which Italian city can you find the marble throne of Attila the Hun?

(1414) Town squares are very popular in Italy and can be found throughout the country. What is the Italian word for a town square?

(1415) What do the following have in common - Aventinus (Aventine), Caelius (Caelian), Capitolium (Capitoline), Esquiliae (Esquiline), Palatium (Palatine), Quirinalis (Quirinal), Viminalis (Viminal)?

(1416) Where in Italy can you find Lago (Lake) Trasimen?

(1417) This city became the capital of the Roman Empire in 402 A.D. and became the seat of power, for a brief period of time, of the Byzantine Empire (eastern Roman Empire) in A.D. 540. This is also the place where Dante completed his renowned work, *The Divine Comedy*. Name this city.

(1418) Italy is the fourth most visited country in the world. What are the top three countries most visited?

(1419) Which region became part of modern-day Italy after World War I?

(1420) What unique Italian building is located in Campo de Miracoli (Field of Miracles)?

(1421) In which Italian city can you find the Aurelian Wall, a defensive wall surrounding this city and built in the late 3rd century A.D.?

(1422) This town was founded by Christians escaping persecution in the 4th century A.D. and became an independent nation in 1243. Name this town/nation.

(1423) 19th century English poets Elizabeth Barrett Browning and Robert Browning lived in Florence for a time. Name their famous home.

(1424) This 13th century structure, built to mathematical and astronomical precision and thus considered one of the most symmetrical in all of Europe, was built by Holy Roman Emperor Frederick II of Hohenstaufen. Name this structure found near Bari in Apulia.

(1425) Which volcano buried the ancient Roman town of Pompeii and the nearby area in A.D. 79?

(1426) This town was originally built on Mount Subasio and was home to Saint Francis. Name this town.

(1427) This town was founded by the Romans as Augusta Praetoria and considered a strategic location near the Alpine passes. Name the town.

(1428) This town was established by the Etruscans and later became the Roman town of Faesulum. Today this town is essentially a suburb overlooking Florence. Name this town.

(1429) This Mediterranean island was subject to the pope for nearly 300 years from the late 1000s to 1312 and subsequently governed by the Italian city-state of Genoa for the next 450 years. In 1768, Genoa sold this island to France, which still governs the island today. Name this island.

TOP 10 OF ITALY

Most Spoken Minority Languages

	LANGUAGE	POPULATION	LOCATION
1	Sardinian	1,269,000	Sardinia
2	Friulian	526,000	Friuli-Venezia-Giulia
3	German	290,000	Trentino-Alto Adige
4	Occitan	178,000	Piedmont. Liguria, Calabria
5	Romany	130,000	Entire Italy
6	Albanian	98,000	Southern Italy, Sicily
7	Franco-Provencal	90,000	Piedmont, Aosta Valley, Apulia
8	Slovenian	70,000	Friuli-Venezia-Giulia
9	Ladin	55,000	Trentino-Alto Adige, Veneto
10	French	20,000	Aosta Valley

(1430) In 1908, an earthquake and resulting tidal wave struck Italy and killed over 100,000 people. This event is one of the worst natural disasters to hit modern Europe. Name the two regions most impacted.

(1431) This city, founded as Mediolanum by the Romans, is the place where Emperor Constantine made his historical edict granting permanent religious freedom to Christians. Today, this city is Italy's leading industrial city and the fashion capital of Italy. Name this city.

(1432) Which Italian city is known for its craft in making glass, including blown glass?

(1433) This place was the ceremonial, legal, social and business center of ancient Rome. Today, it is just a huge complex of ruined temples, basilicas, and arches. What is the name for this place?

(1434) The Calderone Glacier is the southernmost glacier in all of Europe. This glacier sits atop the highest peak in the Apennines, the Corno Grande at 2,912 meters. In which national park is this glacier found?

(1435) Covering approximately 24 square miles, which tiny state, aside from Vatican City, resides within the borders of Italy?

(1436) Which two regions of Italy surround the Republic of San Marino?

(1437) Which two nations border the region of Valle d'Aosta in the north?

(1438) Name the famous bridge with multiple arches and numerous shops that spans the Grand Canal of Venice.

Mileage Distance Chart

ROME									
397	BARI								
350	655	BOLOGNA							
242	662	265	FLORENCE						
467	671	274	206	GENOA					
544	866	198	285	118	MILAN				
192	249	766	457	680	759	NAPLES			
135	933	206	134	357	436	350	PERUGIA		
642	987	319	381	138	122	856	534	TURIN	
484	797	131	235	188	255	709	348	381	VENICE

(1439) This area of southern Italy, extending from Sicily to Naples to Bari, was settled and colonized by the ancient Greeks. Name this area that was arguably the most important Greek colonies outside of Greece.

(1440) Where is the Malpensa airport located?

(1441) Which celebrated Florentine museum contains numerous priceless works of art, including many commissioned by the Medici family?

(1442) How did the winged lion become the symbol of Venice?

(1443) This national park, located in the region of Piedmont, is the largest wilderness area in Italy. Name this national park.

(1444) This town, founded as Arminium by the Romans, is today considered the top destination for tourists on the Adriatic. Name this town.

(1445) During World War II, what significant historical Italian monument was nearly destroyed by the U.S. Army due to the potential threat from snipers?

(1446) Originally established as a military outpost and virtually extinct by 800 A.D., this small town on the coast served as the port of supply to ancient Rome, an inland city. Name this once striving port town.

(1447) Which southern Italian city was nearly destroyed by a massive earthquake in 1909?

(1448) Which town in Italy is known as Piccola Roma (Little Rome) for its importance and strategic location during ancient Roman times?

(1449) Magna Graecia was the name given by the Greeks to their colonized areas in southern Italy and Sicily. What does Magna Graecia mean?

(1450) This town was once the second largest town in Italy and in 216 B.C. allied with Hannibal against Rome. It is also the place where legendary slave Spartacus began his revolt. Name this town.

(1451) Which Italian city is often called La Serenissima, or the most serene and lovely?

(1452) Which region of Italy will add a new province named Fermo, recently approved by voters, in 2009?

(1453) Rome was founded on seven hills, conveniently dubbed the "Seven Hills of Rome". Which hill does legend and archaeology agree that Rome was founded upon and which hill did the capital stand upon?

(1454) What was cited as the top reason Italians are happy to live in Italy?

(1455) This city, founded as Tergeste by the Celts, is the largest port city on the Adriatic Sea. Name this city.

(1456) This town is known for its remarkable 5th century B.C. Vale of Doric temples, considered by many as the best temple examples outside Greece. Name the town.

(1457) The winged lion is the symbol of which Italian city?

(1458) Which nations border Italy?

(1459) What is the name of the gulf of water at the foot of Italy?

(1460) Which Italian university did the monumental Polish astronomer Copernicus attend?

(1461) The ancient Romans called this land Hibernia. Name this present-day country known for its lush green landscape.

(1462) This town was founded by Florentine Cosimo de' Medici in 1571 as a port to circumvent Pisa, an enemy of Florence at the time. Name this coastal town.

(1463) Costa Smeralda (Emerald Coast) is a popular tourist destination for Italians during the summer. Where is this destination hotspot located?

(1464) This town in Sicily is known for the exquisite Roman Villa Imperiale, built by Emperor Maximinianus. Name this town.

(1465) Which famous animals are named after the northern town of Lippiza?

(1466) There are five regions of Italy that have common borders with less than two other regions. Try to name these five regions.

(1467) According to ancient Roman legend, this Tuscan town was founded by the son of Remus, one of the two twins legend says founded Rome. Name this town that began as the Roman military outpost, Sena Julia.

(1468) What is the name of the mighty river that flows through Rome on its way to the sea?

(1469) Spanning the Arno River, the present-day Ponte Vecchio bridge was built in 1345 to replace an old wooden bridge. In which city is this bridge located?

(1470) On which island, located between Sardinia and Tuscany, did Napoleon live in exile from May 1814 to March 1815 before escaping and returning to power, only to meet his demise at the Battle of Waterloo?

(1471) Which area in northern Italy is known for its fertile agricultural land?

IT HAPPENED IN...1912 A.D.

► Over escalating tensions concerning the status of Libya, Italian warships engage the Ottoman Empire and bombard Turkish ports and destroy ships in the Red Sea. Libya soon comes under Italian control.

(1472) This town is the home of Romeo and Juliet and even contains a symbolic tomb near the church where they were said to have married. Name this town.

(1473) This opera house, perhaps the world's greatest theater, opened in Milan in 1778 and can accommodate 2,800 people. Name this opera house.

(1474) Geologically speaking, which region in Italy is the oldest?

(1475) This town, founded as Tibur by the Romans, was once a resort of wealthy Romans and today is known for its magnificent fountains. Name this town.

(1476) This road spanning the western coastline of Italy is considered by many to be one of the most scenic roads in the world. Name this popular road.

(1477) What is the longest river in Italy?

(1478) In which bay are the islands of Ischia and Capri located?

(1479) What is the name of the famous 14th century tower in Siena?

(1480) What is the southernmost major city in Italy?

(1481) The tomb of the great writer Dante, born Durante Alighieri, is located in a city on the Adriatic. To honor him, the area around his tomb observes silence. In which city is his tomb located?

(1482) Along with the town of Pompeii, this town was destroyed by the eruption of Mount Vesuvius in A.D. 79. Name this town.

(1483) In the 15th century, what percentage of the population of Sicily was Jewish?

(1484) This Italian region is named after a Germanic tribe that settled and ruled the land beginning in A.D. 572. Name this northern region.

(1485) What is the only active volcano on the European mainland and when was its last major eruption?

(1486) This town is oftentimes referred to as the center of the Italian Riviera. Name this town.

(1487) Two of the twenty regions of Italy are large islands. Name them.

(1488) The prestigious Nobel Prize is named for Swedish-born Alfred Nobel, born in Stockholm, Sweden. However, in which Italian town did he live and die?

(1489) What is the highest point in Italy?

(1490) Which street in Florence is comparable to Rodeo Drive in Beverly Hills or Michigan Avenue in Chicago?

(1491) This city, founded as Panoramus by the Phoenicians in the 8th century B.C., is considered the world's most conquered city of all time. Name this city.

(1492) What are the Dolomites?

(1493) This ancient Roman structure was originally named the Flavian Amphitheatre and was later renamed for the nearby 130 foot colossus (statue) of the Emperor Nero. Name this structure.

(1494) The Valley of the Temples is one of the most impressive complexes of ancient Greek buildings outside of Greece. In which region is the Valley of the Temples located?

(1495) What was "Mussolinia"?

(1496) This city, once the center of the Roman Empire, is dubbed the "eternal city" and is the home of the Holy Catholic Church. Name this city.

(1497) This Italian region is the largest island in the Mediterranean and its name originated from the ancient Greeks who named the island after the Siculi, the native people of the island. Name this island and Italian region.

(1498) Which landmark in Rome receives over 10 million visitors each year?

(1499) Is Sardinia the largest, second largest or third largest island in the Mediterranean Sea?

(1500) Where in 1940 did Italy experience one of its earliest military defeats of World War II?

(1501) What is the largest metropolitan area by population in Italy?

(1502) Which dubious honor does Mount Etna in Sicily hold?

(1503) What was the original name for the cluster of islands that later become Venice?

(1504) Why was the seat of the Roman Empire transferred to Ravenna from Rome in A.D. 402 by Emperor Honorius?

(1505) This city is home to automakers Ferrari and Maserati. Name this city.

(1506) What is the name of the four islands in Lake Maggiore?

(1507) Founded in 1927, CIT is Italy's national tourist organization. What do the letters represent?

(1508) What is the name of the main canal that winds its way through Venice?

(1509) Approximately what percentage of Italy is considered arable? (a) 15% (b) 22% (c) 28%

(1510) This city was founded by the Etruscans, razed to the ground and rebuilt by the Romans and became the unquestioned center of the Renaissance. Name this city.

(1511) This town, founded by the Corinthians in 734 B.C., was the leading town in Sicily under the Greeks. Name this town.

(1512) Mosaics are pictures made of small pieces of glass or stone and typically used to decorate walls and floors. Name the Italian city dubbed the "city of the mosaics".

(1513) What famed Italian coastal town, located in the Italian Riviera, is due southeast of Genoa?

(1514) Italy is about the same size as which arid western U.S. state?

(1515) This town, located in western Tuscany, is a center of olive oil production and recognized for its imposing town walls. Name this town.

(1516) What is the awe-inspiring cathedral in Florence that is the fourth largest cathedral in Europe?

(1517) Although this island in the Mediterranean Sea is not part of Italy, it remains linguistically and culturally Italian. Name this island.

(1518) This town was once a major city of the Etruscans and later renamed Arretium by the Romans. Name this town.

(1519) In which region is the city of Milan located?

(1520) This city, founded as Neapolis in 750 B.C. by the Greeks, is known for their pizza and espresso. Name this city.

(1521) What is the regional capital of Sardinia?

(1522) How many residents died in Pompeii when Mount Vesuvius erupted on August 24, A.D. 79?

(1523) Naples is the capital and most prominent city of which region located south of the Lazio region?

(1524) After who is Saint Peter's Cathedral in Rome named?

(1525) Sicily and Sardinia are the two largest islands of Italy. Which is the third largest island?

(1526) This town is said to contain the actual ancient house of the Virgin Mary, transported here in 1294 from Nazareth. Name this town.

(1527) Where can you find the Lido, Giudecca Canal, and Ponte Della Liberta?

(1528) Which naval base in Italy is the home port for the United States Navy's Sixth Fleet?

(1529) This British capital was founded by the Romans in 115 A.D. as Londinium. Name the modern city.

(1530) Naples was founded by the ancient Greeks and given the name "Neapolis". What does this mean in Greek?

(1531) What mighty river runs through both Florence and Pisa?

(1532) In which Italian city would you find the remains of Saint Nicholas of Myra, the patron saint of Russia?

(1533) In Latin, the word for this place means "tellers of the future". During ancient Roman times, the location where this place now sits was once home to fortunetellers. What stands on this location today?

Nobel Prize Winners

	ITALIAN	YEAR	CATEGORY
1	Giosuè Carducci	1906	Literature
2	Camillo Golgi	1906	Medicine
3	Ernesto T. Moneta	1907	Peace
4	Guglielmo Marconi	1909	Physics
5	Grazia Deledda	1926	Literature
6	Luigi Pirandello	1934	Literature
7	Enrico Fermi	1938	Physics
8	Daniel Bovet	1957	Medicine
9	Salvatore Quasimodo	1959	Literature
10	Emilio Gino Segrè	1959	Physics
11	Giulio Natta	1963	Chemistry
12	Salvador E. Luria	1969	Medicine
13	Eugenio Montale	1975	Literature
14	Renato Dulbecco	1975	Medicine
15	Carlo Rubbia	1984	Physics
16	Franco Modigliani	1985	Economics
17	Rita Levi-Montalcini	1986	Medicine
18	Dario Fò	1997	Literature
19	William D. Phillips	1997	Physics
20	Riccardo Giacconi	2002	Physics

(1534) This hilltop town of Umbria was known as Volsinii by its Etruscan founders. Underneath the town in caves you can find ancient 9th century B.C. Etruscan settlements. Today, this town is known for their excellent wines. Name this town.

(1535) What straight divides Sicily from Calabria and the rest of Italy?

(1536) Which famous Italian lake is shaped like an upside down letter "y"?

(1537) How many Italian cities have populations of over one million and which cities are they?

(1538) This town is known as the first city to emerge from the dark ages and has a coastline and road named after it. Name this town.

(1539) This Italian town was home to the world's greatest violin makers of all time - Stradivari, Amati and Guarneri families. Name this town.

(1540) This town, known for superb wine and olive production, overlooks Rome and was originally founded as Tusculum by the Latins. Name this town.

(1541) How many regions are in Italy?

(1542) William Shakespeare wrote five plays that are set in Italy. Name these plays.

(1543) Where in Italy would you find the Capo di Santa Maria de Leuca, a place where many Italians visit to relax in the many stunning vistas?

(1544) What is the name of the beautiful gardens in Florence near Forte di Belvedere?

(1545) This city, founded as a safe haven for people fleeing barbarians after the fall of Rome, is known for its canals and 118 tiny islets. Name this city.

(1546) Only two regions in Italy have common borders with six other regions. Name these two regions.

(1547) To which region of Italy would you travel to if you wanted to visit the Italian Riviera? (Hint: Portofino)

(1548) This Italian city, nicknamed La Superba (the proud), lies due north of the Ligurian Sea. It was sacked by Hannibal on this way to Rome in the Punic Wars and is the largest port city in Italy and second largest in the Mediterranean. Name this city.

(1549) This city in Tuscany is known for their Corsa del Palio - banner contests and horse races - and was a major rival of Florence during the Renaissance. Name this city.

(1550) Which major mountain chain runs through the central heart of Italy?

(1551) The Egyptian obelisk in front of the Church of Santa Maria Novella in Florence was at one time used for what purpose?

(1552) Which tiny European nation, known for their affluent accommodations and gambling, was founded as a colony of Genoa in 1215?

(1553) The city of Trieste lies in the northeastern part of Italy. Name the country that practically surrounds the city.

(1554) Which tower, nicknamed El Paron de Casa, provides a glorious view of Venice and its lagoon and is considered a defining symbol of the city?

> ## IT HAPPENED IN... 1870 A.D.
>
> ▶ **French troops are withdrawn from Rome to support in the Franco-Prussian War. After a short bombardment, Italian forces enter and liberate Rome. Italy is reunited after 1,500 years.**

(1555) This city, founded by the Taurini Gauls in 28 B.C. and later renamed Augusta Taurinorum by the Romans, is considered the center of Italy's automotive industry and is the headquarters of automaker Fiat. This city hosted the 2006 Winter Olympic games and its name means "Little Bull" in Italian. Name this Piedmontese city.

(1556) Approximately how many lakes can be found in Italy?

(1557) Today, the Ponte Vecchio bridge in Florence is a bustling place with many jewelers selling their merchandise. However, what was the original use of the Ponte Vecchio?

(1558) This town was founded by the Etruscans on a hilltop and was the setting for the movie *Under the Tuscan Sun*. Name this town.

(1559) What is the largest lake in Italy?

(1560) This city, founded as Zancle by the Greeks, was devastated in 1908 by an earthquake and tidal wave that killed over 80,000 people. Name this city.

(1561) In which Italian city can you find two "leaning towers" standing next to each other?

(1562) This town in Tuscany is sometimes called the "city of towers" and considered by many as the best preserved medieval hill town in all of Europe. This town grew from being on the main pilgrim route from northern Europe to Rome. Name this town.

(1563) Florence is the capital of which Italian region?

(1564) This city is known for its world famous leaning tower and is the birthplace of Galileo. Name this town.

(1565) This town is the home of Parmesan cheese and a ham that bears its name. Name this town.

(1566) Cortina was part of what empire before the end of World War I?

(1567) This town, founded as Taras by the Spartans of Greece in 708 B.C., was a major center of Magna Garecia and is well known for its wild dance, the tarantella. Name this town.

(1568) This town was formed when Mussolini merged Porto Maurizio and Oneglia with the aim of building a new vibrant city mirroring those of the north. Name this town.

(1569) The city of Florence was called Florentia by the Romans. What did the word Florentia mean to the Romans?

(1570) The Straight of Bonifacio is located between two large islands, one Italian and one French, in the Mediterranean Sea. Name these islands.

(1571) The ancient ruin of Pompeii is located next to which major present-day Italian city?

(1572) Ernest Hemingway lived in many locations throughout Europe. One such place was a country inn named Locanda Cipriani on a tiny island near Venice. Name this island.

(1573) This town contains the famous ancient Etruscan necropolis of the "Tomb of Shields and Chairs" and "Tomb of the Capitals". Name this town.

(1574) Opened in 1792, Teatro La Fenice is one of the most renowned theaters in Europe. In which city can you find this theater meaning "The Phoenix" in English?

(1575) The Promontorio del Gargano is a mountainous location dotted with many ancient ruins. Where in Italy can you find this location?

(1576) This Italian town is internationally famous for its white marble quarries where distinguished sculptors selected their marble. Michelangelo even hand-picked the marble for his sculptures here, including what was used to sculpt the *David* statue. Name this town located in Tuscany.

(1577) This city was founded by the Etruscans as Felsina and served as their capital. It was later renamed Bononia by the Gauls and today is sometimes called the "Flemish City". Name this city.

(1578) The Lanterna is considered the first lighthouse built after the Great Lighthouse of Alexandria, a wonder of the ancient world. Where was the Laterna lighthouse located?

(1579) During the Middle Ages, this region of Italy marked the edge of the Holy Roman Empire. As a result, the name of this region is derived from the word for "border area". Name this region.

(1580) Which beautiful German city, located on the eastern banks of the Rhine River, was founded by the Romans during the first century B.C. as Colonia Claudia Ara Agrippinensis (also known as Agrippina Romanorum)?

(1581) Where can you find the Pollino National Park?

(1582) Which Italian city was the capital of Italy during the period 1865-1870?

(1583) Which Hungarian city was founded by the Romans in the 1st century A.D.?

(1584) This island, located outside of Venice, is known for producing the most beautiful and delicate glass in all of Europe and has been doing so for over a thousand years. Name this island and the glass that bears its name.

(1585) Which five of the twenty regions of Italy, due to historic and ethnic reasons, are extended special autonomy?

(1586) In the 4th century B.C., exiles from the Greek colonies of Magna Graecia colonized this region of Italy. The northern most point of Greek influence on the Italian peninsula extended to the town of Ancona in this region. Name this region.

(1587) Which city in southern Italy was founded by the ancient Phoenicians? (Hint: capital of a region of Italy)

(1588) This city, Italy's largest port city, traded with the Phoenicians and Greeks before the 6th century B.C. and is the birthplace of Christopher Columbus. Name this city.

NAME THE REGION

(1589) In which part of Sicily can you find the best-preserved Greek temples and Doic columns?

(1590) #1 - Name this region. (Hint: capital is L'Aquila)

(1591) #2 - Name this region. (Hint: capital is Aosta)

(1592) #3 - Name this region. (Hint: capital is Bari)

(1593) #4 - Name this region. (Hint: capital is Potenza)

(1594) #5 - Name this region. (Hint: capital is Catanzaro)

(1595) #6 - Name this region. (Hint: capital is Naples)

1984 A.D. ▶ Catholicism no longer the state religion of Italy

(1596) #7 - Name this region. (Hint: capital is Bologna)

(1597) #8 - Name this region. (Hint: capital is Trieste)

(1598) # 9 - Name this region. (Hint: capital is Rome)

(1599) #10 - Name this region. (Hint: capital is Genoa)

(1600) #11 - Name this region. (Hint: capital is Milan)

(1601) #12 - Name this region. (Hint: capital is Ancona)

(1602) #13 - Name this region. (Hint: capital is Campobasso)

(1603) #14 - Name this region. (Hint: capital is Turin)

(1604) #15 - Name this region. (Hint: capital is Cagliari)

(1605) #16 - Name this region. (Hint: capital is Palermo)

(1606) #17 - Name this region. (Hint: capital is Trento)

(1607) #18 - Name this region. (Hint: capital is Florence)

(1608) #19 - Name this region. (Hint: capital is Perugia)

(1609) #20 - Name this region. (Hint: capital is Venice)

CHAPTER 13

CHAPTER
F·O·U·R·T·E·E·N
XIV

WORLD RANKINGS

How Italy Ranks Against the World

"When you build bridges, you can keep crossing them."

- **RICK PITINO**

"The real problem is what to do with the problem-solvers after the problems are solved."

- **GAY TALESE**

175

(1610) Where does Italy rank in the world for most winners of the Nobel Prize for literature? (a) 1st (b) 3rd (c) 6th (d) 12th

(1611) Where does Italy rank in the world for biggest producers of fruit? (a) 6th (b) 14th (c) 24th (d) 38th

(1612) Where does Italy rank in the world for most medal winners in the summer Olympics? (a) 5th (b) 9th (c) 19th (d) 22nd

(1613) How does Italy compare against the rest of the European nations with regards to birthrate?

(1614) Where does Italy rank in the world for the total amount of coffee consumed annually? (a) 1st (b) 5th (c) 11th (d) 17th

(1615) Where does Italy rank in the world for most medal winners in the Winter Olympics? (a) 1st (b) 2nd (c) 9th (d) 17th

(1616) Where does Italy rank in the world for largest economies? (a) 4th (b) 10th (c) 12th (d) 24th

(1617) Where does Italy rank in the world for most doctors per person? (a) 1st (b) 5th (c) 19th (d) 27th

(1618) Where does Italy rank in the world for most police per person? (a) 3rd (b) 12th (c) 23rd (d) 57th

(1619) Where does Italy rank in the world for most wine consumed per person? (a) 1st (b) 2nd (c) 3rd (d) 6th

(1620) Where does Italy rank in Europe for most densely populated countries? (a) 1st (b) 3rd (c) 5th (d) 9th

(1621) Where does Italy rank in the world for longest road networks? (a) 2nd (b) 11th (c) 21st (d) 36th

(1622) Where does Italy rank in the world for most tomatoes produced per year? (a) 1st (b) 4th (c) 15th (d) 26th

(1623) Where does Italy rank in the world for most crowded roads? (a) 1st (b) 15th (c) 23rd (d) 31st

(1624) Where does Italy rank in the world for largest populations? (a) 22nd (b) 33rd (c) 39th (d) 51st

(1625) Where does Italy rank in the world for longest railway networks? (a) 17th (b) 27th (c) 37th (d) 47th

(1626) Where does Italy rank in the world for highest median age? (a) 1st (b) 2nd (c) 9th (d) 17th

(1627) Where does Italy rank in the world for the nation most visited by tourists? (a) 1st (b) 2nd (c) 4th (d) 7th

(1628) Where does Italy rank in the world for highest life expectancy? (a) 2nd (b) 5th (c) 11th (d) 16th

(1629) Where does Italy rank in the world for foreign donations of aid? (a) 3rd (b) 7th (c) 12th (d) 22nd

(1630) Where does Italy rank in the world for largest manufacturing output? (a) 6th (b) 12th (c) 23rd (d) 47th

CHAPTER
F·I·F·T·E·E·N

TRIVIA ANSWERS TO ALL TRIVIA QUESTIONS

"A hunch is creativity trying to tell you something."

- FRANK CAPRA

"The difference between the impossible and the possible lies in a person's determination."

- TOMMY LASORDA

Chapter 1: *Astronomy, Exploration, and Transportation*

(1) Santa Maria, Nina and Pinta

(2) John Cabot, born Giovanni Caboto (1450 - 1498)

(3) Only one, black. This was in response to gondoliers painting their gondolas many different colors, thus detracting from the environment.

(4) One-way street

(5) Pineapples

(6) They begin with the street name followed by the address number

(7) Trinidad

(8) Autostrada

(9) Giovanni da Verrazano (1483 - 1528)

(10) The names for Christopher Columbus in Spanish and in Portuguese, respectively

(11) Gondola, piloted by a gondolier

(12) Fall of Granada, the final stronghold of the Moors in Spain, thus fueling nationalistic fervor.

(13) Although Columbus became the first European to sight the continent of South America on his third voyage to the New

World in 1498, it was Amerigo Vespucci that first set foot there in 1499.

(14) Taxi, as in taxicab

(15) Four - in 1492, 1493, 1498, and 1502

(16) Leonardo da Vinci International Airport

(17) Bartholomew Columbus, the brother of Christopher Columbus

(18) Honduras, Panama, Venezuela and perhaps Florida, although this claim is disputed.

(19) France

(20) Island of San Salvador (also known as Watling Island) in the Bahamas

(21) Water bus in Venice

(22) Alt & Avanti

(23) Christopher Columbus. Similar to how Americans celebrate Columbus Day

(24) England

(25) Three - University Library of Pavia, Santo Domingo in the Dominican Republic and Santiago de Compostella

(26) China

(27) Christopher Columbus. He brought them back from the New World

(28) Columbia, South America

(29) Andrea Doria

(30) Amerigo Vespucci (1454 - 1512)

(31) Always Spanish and never Italian

(32) Argentina and Brazil

(33) Amerigo Vespucci, sailed for the Spanish and Portuguese

(34) 17th century

(35) Amerigo Vespucci

(36) Venezuela, which means "Little Venice" in the Venetian dialect

(37) Metro subway transit station

(38) Giovanni da Verrazano

(39) (c) New York. The monument, both pedestal and statue, stands 75 feet tall

(40) Milan and Rome, where the subway system is called the Metropolitana

(41) Eastern coast of Canada

(42) Cape Cod

(43) Marco Polo (1254 - 1324)

(44) Christopher Columbus. Upon returning to the New World one year after its founding, he found Isabella destroyed by native islanders.

(45) Via Appia

(46) Italy's fastest passenger train

(47) Marco Polo (1254 - 1324)

(48) Around 170 B.C.

(49) French. Christopher Columbus used this book as a reference for his travels.

(50) Piracy, for the French against the Spanish

(51) Blue for highways and green for main roads

(52) Chartmaker

Chapter 2: *Cuisine & Culinary Contributions*

(53) Sfogliatelle

(54) Pretzel, (crisscross pretzel)

(55) Sardinia

(56) Prosecco

(57) Bernardo Buontalenti

(58) Espresso or cappuccino

(59) Colazione

(60) Cannoli

(61) Resveratrol, small molecules found in the skin of red grapes

(62) Espresso

(63) White truffles

(64) Saracens (Arabs)

(65) Ice cream cone

(66) Tuscany

(67) Antipasto

(68) In most of southern Italy, lasagna is made with tomato sauce and ricotta - or tomato sauce and meatballs - and can be found made with fish - or made with greens and vegetables. However, in many parts of northern Italy, lasagna is served in the winter - made with Sugo alla Bolognese and béchamel sauce, and an abundant dusting of grated cheese before heating.

(69) Fava bean

(70) Cantaloupe sherbet

(71) Soft and creamy cheese

(72) Tiramisu

(73) Apulia

(74) Brooklyn, New York

(75) Little worms

(76) Table wine

(77) Plural of the Italian word spaghetto, which is a diminutive of spago, meaning string, twine or literally little strings.

(78) Traditional coffee served in the United States and drank rarely by Italians

(79) Amaretto (Amaretto di Saronno)

(80) Balsamic vinegar

(81) Refers to the method of preparing a rice dish rather than the rice itself. Risotto is typically made of Arborio rice and seasoned with saffron.

(82) Abruzzese panarda

(83) Al dente

(84) Gelato

(85) Valpolicella

(86) Cicoria

(87) Only authentic Italian cooking is used

(88) Ghirardelli, founded by Domingo Ghirardelli

(89) Well done on the bottom and slightly under-cooked on the top.

(90) Water - drinking undiluted wine was considered bad manners.

(91) Modena and Reggio

(92) Panforte

(93) Poor man's food

(94) Nebbiolo

(95) The meatball

(96) Linguine

(97) Invented tomato sauce and perfected its use

(98) Sardinia

(99) Fish

(100) Galliano

(101) Pizza Sicilian

(102) Tomatoes

(103) Vincenza

(104) Marsala, from the town of the same name

(105) Filet Mignon

(106) Coffee Arabica, commonly known as Arabica

(107) Pizzelle iron

(108) Asti

(109) Asia Minor (present-day Turkey)

(110) Pizza Margherita

(111) Pizza

(112) American soldiers returning from Italy after World War II

(113) Wine, of course

(114) Olive oil

(115) Red wine

(116) Italian bacon

(117) Calabria

(118) Homemade food

(119) Caesar salad

(120) Fork, which Italians invented

(121) Over 200

(122) You never age at the dinner table

(123) Naples, pizza king of the world

(124) Genoa

(125) Centerbe

(126) Baby octopus

(127) Spinach

(128) Burns at a higher temperature than other oils

(129) Chianti, pronounced Ki-ANN-tee

(130) Pre-dates even the ancient Romans

(131) Pappardelle

(132) All fruit

(133) Salt cod

(134) Sausage, made with pork, garlic, spices, salt and seasoned with pepper

(135) Pasta

(136) For each variety they are practically identical except for their shape. Italian bread is shorter and plumper while French bread is longer and skinnier - a baguette. Some places in northern Italy serve bread that resembles French bread.

(137) House wine

(138) Priests hats

(139) Polenta

(140) Ancient Persia, via ancient Greek colonists from Magna Graecia

(141) Michetti

(142) Sharp blue cheese that bears its name

(143) Venice, in 1654

(144) Butter

(145) Liguria

(146) Panettone

(147) Snow mixed with honey for a sweetener

(148) 9%, nearly triple cow's milk

(149) Saffron

(150) Bruschetta

(151) Culatelli

(152) Water buffalo

(153) Seafood salad

(154) Vendemmia

(155) Waiter

(156) Cappuccino in the morning and espresso after meals

(157) In wicker-wrapped fiaschi

(158) Vermouth

(159) Olives must not touch the ground and become soiled

(160) Curly endive

(161) Standing up

(162) Glass bottle used to hold wine

(163) Small cup used to drink espresso

(164) Insalata caprese, or simply caprese

(165) Clams

(166) Fruit

(167) Broccoli

(168) From the brown hooded frock worn by the Capuchin monks

(169) Bologna and Naples

(170) White wine produced in the region of Piedmont

(171) Pasta

(172) Cooked "In the Oven"

(173) Grappa at 20% of the Italian spirits market and whisky with 15%

(174) Beer

(175) Zabaglione

(176) Spumone, called spumoni in the United States

(177) Pesto

(178) Turin (Torino)

(179) Barista

(180) Brunello di Montalcino

(181) Italian ice cream parlor

(182) Compari and lemoncello, in that order

(183) Espresso

(184) One eats well in Bologna

(185) Etruscan men ate with their children and wives, while Roman men did not.

(186) Gelato, he is considered the father of Italian gelato

(187) Standard tap water

(188) Superior Parmigiano-Reggiano and lower-quality Grana

(189) Mustard

(190) Delicious little balls of dough covered with honey and sprinkles

(191) Basil

(192) Bresaola

(193) Black mussels

(194) Pasta made of potato, or potato dumplings

(195) Espresso or cappuccino with a shot of grappa or sambucca added to "correct" it.

(196) Best described as a combination between the two.

(197) Served smothered in cheese

(198) Etruscans

(199) Extra virgin olive oil

(200) Grappa

(201) Waffle

(202) Perugia

(203) Artichoke

(204) Biscotti

(205) Cherry trees

(206) Love, happiness and prosperity

(207) Tripolini

(208) Venice

(209) That the wine meets established standards established by the Italian government. These standards include, but are not limited to taste, color, acidity, aroma, alcohol content and longevity. Wine labels with the imprint DOCG means garantita, or guaranteed to meet these standards.

(210) Either Spaghetti alla Bolognese or simply ragu

(211) Fertile soils surrounding Mount Etna in Sicily

(212) Mostaccioli

(213) Cassata

(214) Anchovies

(215) Chianti

(216) Zeppole di San Giuseppe

(217) Biscuit that is very popular in Naples

(218) Extra virgin olive oil contains less acidity than virgin olive oil

(219) Italian omelet

(220) Tomato. And yes, tomatoes are technically a fruit and not a vegetable

(221) Nutmeg

(222) Largest pasta factory in the world

(223) Minestrone

(224) Evergreen

(225) Spaghetti was made with "durum" wheat, which was not produced in China at the time of Marco Polo.

(226) Miscela (blend), macinazione (grind), macchina (machine), and mano (hand)

(227) Because it took nearly 200 years for tomatoes to reach Italy from Spain after the Spanish conquistador Cortez brought them back from Mexico in 1519.

(228) Stuffed eggplant

(229) Tomato

Chapter 3: *Economics, Money, & Business*

---

(230) Fiat

(231) Costa Cruise Lines

(232) Marine insurance

(233) Germany and France, 18% and 11.5% of total imports, respectively

(234) Bank

(235) Ducats in Venice and Florins in Florence

(236) Fabbrica Italiana Automobili Torino

(237) Velvet

(238) Russia and Algeria

(239) Fiat

(240) .IT

(241) Tabacchi

(242) Initiative to grow more wheat started by Mussolini

(243) Siena

(244) Venice

(245) Lombardy

(246) World's oldest surviving map from the 1st century B.C. by a previously obscure geographer, Artemidorus of Ephesus.

(247) Letter of Credit

(248) Lamborghini

(249) Auto manufacturing

(250) Gold coin, called the florin

(251) Lombard Street

(252) Mercury

(253) Motorcycle

(254) Euro

(255) Hydro-electric power

(256) Germany, at nearly 14% of goods and services exported

(257) Florence

(258) 20%

(259) Lamborghini, Ferrari and Maserati

(260) Increase GDP by 0.2% annually over the next four years

(261) Cloth and silk manufacturing

(262) Lombardy, Piedmont and Liguria

(263) Peroni and Maretti

(264) (c) 60%

(265) Alitalia

(266) Vespa

(267) (c) 85%

(268) Horse with its two front legs raised

(269) 2002

(270) Valuation analysis for the financial markets

(271) (d) Milan, Rome is second

(272) Anonima Lombarda Fabbrica Automobili (Lombard Automobile Factory)

(273) (a) cars

(274) 72 out of 100 people

(275) Services industry, larger by a 4 to 1 ratio

(276) Transport salt inland from the Mediterranean Sea to Rome

(277) Replaced the Greek process of heating and stamping with their invention of molten molding.

(278) Lira

(279) Libra abbreviated as lb. meaning pound

Chapter 4: *Holidays, Traditions, & People*

(280) Traditional Italian card games

(281) Ancient Romans

(282) Buona Pasqua

(283) Rome and Turin

(284) Peace

(285) Maria Montessori (1870 - 1952)

(286) Tarantella

(287) Point of entry into Europe for illegal immigrants

(288) Pasquetta

(289) Trentino-Alto Adige

(290) Easter season

(291) Italian hospitality focusing on the enjoyment of good company, good food and good drink.

(292) Confetti and confection

(293) Muslims

(294) (b) 10%. Swiss of French heritage make up 18%.

(295) United States. He was offered a commission by President Abraham Lincoln during the American Civil War.

(296) Remus and Romulus

(297) "buono come il pane", or as good as bread

(298) More than one million

(299) Toronto

(300) Tribe of Itali, an ancient country and people of southern Italy

(301) Wishing and then pulling apart a wishbone

(302) Liberation Day

(303) Trevi fountain, known as the fountain of love

(304) Albanian, Moroccan and Romanian, in that order

(305) Breaking a mirror

(306) 753 B.C.

(307) Labor Day

(308) Luciano Pavarotti (1935 - present)

(309) Green is for liberty and hope, white is for virtue and faith and red is for courage and charity.

(310) Sacred niches or small roadside shrines along Italian roads

(311) Italian National Anthem, known as *L'Inno di Mameli*

(312) Corsa del Palio, or Parade of the Banner

(313) Age 14

(314) *La Raspa*

(315) Dog

(316) Prior to his execution, Saint Valentine wrote a letter to a friend and signed the letter with the salutation, Your Valentine.

(317) Fig

(318) Lombardy with the most and Val d'Aosta with the least

(319) Renaissance music, culture, food and costumes

(320) Saint Joseph's Day

(321) Attachment to one's village or birthplace, something strongly felt by Italians.

(322) Leonardo da Vinci (1452 - 1519)

(323) La Befana

(324) Carnevale

(325) To keep gladiators from retreating to corners and to allow the spectators a closer view of the action.

(326) Lupercalia, the Roman festival of love with a fertility rite of honor

(327) 300

(328) 14 to 19 years old

(329) Protestants who have been living in Italy before the time of the Reformation.

(330) I'Pupi

(331) Because legend says that brother Romulus killed Remus, thus

Rome was named after the surviving brother.

(332) *Little Drummer Boy*

(333) 250,000

(334) Between 150,000 and 200,000

(335) Six-sided dice

(336) The goat

(337) Blacksmith

(338) Coperta

(339) Italian Christmas tree

(340) Etruscans

(341) Certificate of citizenship

(342) Galileo Galilei (1564 - 1642)

(343) Evening event where people stroll down the streets to socialize and look good

(344) Full-face veils and burqas

(345) First Italian to be knighted

(346) Prepared religious sacrifices and tended to the sacred fires

(347) During ancient Roman times, people believed that lovebirds began mating on February 14th.

(348) Venus

(349) February, prior to the start of Lent

(350) Inherited the practice from the Jews

(351) New York and Buenos Aires

(352) Jews who have resided in Italy for well over 2,000 years

(353) Neptune

(354) 80%

(355) Christmas, meaning Merry Christmas

(356) Toast

(357) San Paulo

(358) Cats

(359) Forum

(360) A huge celebration event was hosted at the Roman Colosseum where 2,000 gladiators and over 200 wild animals were said to have died.

(361) Christopher Columbus

(362) Michelangelo

(363) (1) Pieta - respect for elders, ancestors and religion; (2) Continentia - self-control; (3) Aequitas - equanimity and impartiality; (4) Virtus - manliness, or proper conduct becoming a man or soldier; (5) Fides - the obligation to be faithful to one's word.

(364) Wooden sword

(365) Galileo Galilei

(366) Cupid

(367) Cats

(368) Benvenuto Cellini (1500 - 1571), a goldsmith and sculptor, who wrote *The Life of Benvenuto Cellini*

(369) Tax levied to encourage single men to wed as soon as possible

(370) Venice and the coastal town of Viareggio

(371) Killing of slaves on their chieftain's grave

(372) Jupiter

(373) Niccolo Machiavelli (1469 - 1527)

(374) New Year's Day

(375) Scopa

(376) Fortuna

(377) He was a vegetarian - a result of his love for animals. He was even known to buy pigeons just to set them free.

(378) Bath, England

(379) Spain, followed by France and then Britain

(380) 90%

(381) Archaeology

(382) Aventurina (Venetian dialect), or avventurina in Italian

(383) Health, wealth, happiness, fertility, and longevity

(384) Pronto

(385) Some Sicilians are decedents of the Normans and the Longobardi (Lombards), a Germanic tribe

(386) Spoleto

(387) Six

> **Chapter 5:** Holy Catholic Church & the Vatican

(388) Saint Peter. A nearby plaque reads "Thou art Peter, and upon this rock I will build my church".

(389) Jesuit Order

(390) Holy Catholic Church

(391) *The Jeweler's Shop*

(392) Adolph Hitler

(393) Airplanes are restricted from flying over the Vatican

(394) Secret ballot

(395) Early Christian burial places

(396) Laid railroad tracks for the Long Island Railroad

(397) Peter's Pence

(398) Issued by the pope, a Papal Bull is a written statement bearing the pope's official seal.

(399) Jesuit Order

(400) Saint Francis of Assisi (1181 - 1226). His feast day is celebrated on October 4th.

(401) Christian relic

(402) Churches of Florence

(403) Avignon, then part of the Kingdom of Naples and now part of modern-day France

(404) Marks on the feet and hands that resemble the crucifixion of Jesus Christ.

(405) Burned. The smoke is released to signal whether or not a new pope was elected.

(406) Branch of an olive tree brought back by a dove

(407) Saint John the Baptist

(408) Queen Christina of Sweden

(409) Saint Francis of Assisi (1181 - 1226)

(410) Blessed Virgin Mary, the mother of Jesus Christ

(411) Michelangelo, in response to a question of how much longer he will take before completing the Sistine Chapel.

(412) Advanced the then current date by ten days - from October 4th to October 15th.

(413) Basilica of Santa Maria Maggiore

(414) Saint Peter

(415) Ambassador of the pope

(416) Campanile

(417) Saint Clare of Assisi

(418) Sacred Heart in Rome

(419) Iuesus Nazarenus Rex Iudaeorum, or Jesus of Nazareth, King of the Jews

(420) Shroud of Turin

(421) Saint Valentine

(422) Savior

(423) He drafted, signed and had notarized a letter resigning from the Papacy. Thus, the pope would not be arrested, only a common citizen.

(424) Trent (Trento)

(425) Il Poverello

(426) 1931, first broadcasted by Guglielmo Marconi, the inventor of the radio, who introduced Pope Pius XI.

(427) White line on the pavement

(428) Saint Peter

(429) *Acta Apostolicae Sedis*

(430) Containers of his own blood for emergency situations. He had a rare blood type.

(431) Saint John the Baptist (San Giovanni) - feast day is celebrated on June 24th

(432) Saint Theodore

(433) Theodosius I

(434) Twice

(435) First woman buried at Saint Peter's Basilica

(436) Granted freedom of worship to Christians and gave them special privileges to motivate conversion of others to Christianity.

(437) State of Vatican City

(438) Saint James (San Gioacomo)

(439) Swiss Guard

(440) Red is symbolic of one's willingness to shed blood for his faith

(441) Christians refused to worship the Roman emperor as a god

(442) No, but in 1981 he did refuse a $2 million inheritance from an Italian lady, known as "Mamma Rosa"

(443) 39 languages!

(444) (c) 456 years

(445) Castel Gandolfo

(446) Saint Pietro - feast day is celebrated on June 29th

(447) San Francisco

(448) Apostolic Palace

(449) Pikes or halberds

(450) Santa Lucia (Saint Lucy), born in Sicily

(451) Soviet dictator Joseph Stalin on learning that the Vatican would not stoop to Hitler's demands during World War II.

(452) Polish, German, Italian, Spanish, English and French

(453) Veronica's Veil

(454) Saint Thomas Aquinas (1225 - 1274)

(455) That Naples will be saved from disaster. When it didn't happen in 1941, Mount Vesuvius erupted.

(456) Friars Minor

(457) Sacred College of Cardinals

(458) Monsignor

(459) Jesuit Order

(460) Saint Francis of Assisi (1181 - 1226)

(461) Church of San Domenico in Naples

(462) Saint Francis of Assisi

(463) None, Vatican City has no income tax

(464) Aramaic. Jesus did read the Scriptures in Hebrew however.

(465) Yes. Saint Peter, a disciple of Jesus and the first pope, and Pope Anacletus II, who had a great-grandfather of Jewish heritage.

(466) Saint Francis of Assisi

(467) Italian

(468) Begun on May 8, 1508 and ended on October 31, 1512

(469) Don Novello, who played Father Guido Sarducci on the television comedy Saturday Night Live.

(470) Swiss Guard

(471) Straw

(472) Image of the cross

(473) Christianity

(474) Ecclesiastical Latin

(475) Free ferry crossings over the river Po for life

(476) Messina

(477) Pope John Paul II

(478) *Ave Maria*

(479) That Easter Sunday would fall on the first Sunday after the full moon and the cross was made the official symbol of Christianity.

(480) "Farewell to meat" - the period prior to lent

(481) 1999

(482) Portugal

(483) Saint Peter's Square, Vatican City

(484) Baltimore

(485) Zucchetto

(486) During the feast of Saturnalia from December 17th through December 23rd, gifts were exchanged to honor the god Saturn.

(487) Saint Agatha

(488) Saint Benedict of Nursia (480 - 543)

(489) Saint Ambrose

(490) Wolf

(491) (c) 1626

(492) Fish

(493) Karol Wojtyla

(494) No salary, nor a bank account

(495) Saint Scholastica

(496) Secretary of state

(497) Once every five years

(498) Saint Peter's Basilica, Vatican City

(499) "God Bless You"

(500) Padre Pio, a Catholic priest

(501) Saint Anthony of Padua

(502) Saint Ambrose

(503) Saint Francis of Assisi

(504) Baptism, penance, communion, confirmation, marriage, ordination and last rites

(505) Pope John Paul II, a big soccer fan

(506) Two years, nine months and two days. Pope Gregory X was elected on September 1, 1271

(507) *The Last Judgment*, painted on the entire wall behind the alter in the Sistine Chapel

(508) While a boy in Poland, he was hit by a truck and not found until the next morning in a ditch. The accident fractured his skull.

(509) Vision of Christ told him to return to Rome, the place where he was later martyred

(510) Saint Thomas Aquinas (1225 - 1274)

(511) To oversee rituals and ceremonies performed by the Pope

(512) Pontius Pilate. Each spoke in different languages with the help of a translator. Jesus spoke Aramaic and Pilate spoke Latin.

(513) Daily Vatican newspaper distributed to over 100 nations

(514) Latin

Chapter 6: *Government, Organization, & Leadership*

---

(515) Republic Day

(516) Last of the Roman emperors in the west as the Roman Empire was forever conquered in 476 A.D. by barbarians led by Odocer.

(517) Milan

(518) None, the postwar constitution separates Church and State

(519) Italian National Anthem

(520) Nearly 1,500 years until reunification in the 19th century.

(521) Augustus (63 B.C. - 14 A.D.), the name given to Octavian, or Octavious, by the Roman Senate.

(522) 1947, during post-World War II reconstruction

(523) Turin

(524) Approximately 50 million people, with over 1.5 million people in Rome alone

(525) Umberto II

(526) Cicero

(527) People who fled Italy when Mussolini and the Fascists came to power.

(528) (a) 5'7" - Germany's Hitler was only 5'8"

(529) The Leader

(530) Seven

(531) Italian president

(532) Count Camillo di Cavour

(533) Turin and Florence

(534) Genoa

(535) October 31, 1922

(536) Julius Caesar (102 - 44 B.C.)

(537) To promote union

(538) 54%

(539) *The Agony and the Ecstasy*

(540) Lorenzo de' Medici, or Lorenzo the Magnificent, who ruled from 1469 to 1492

(541) Both saints were physicians and the Medici name means physician or doctor.

(542) 15. Under the current system, five judges are appointed by the president, five by the parliament and five by the highest law and administrative courts.

(543) Comune

(544) Rebel militia seeking to unify Italy

(545) Communism and socialism

(546) Improving schools, building patriotism and eradicating malaria by draining swamps and marshes

(547) Roman common law, or "ius comune gentium"

(548) Emperor Justinian, technically an emperor of the eastern Roman Empire

(549) Mussolini

(550) Benito Mussolini (1893 - 1945), so named by his parents after the Mexican revolutionary Juarez

(551) Parliament

(552) General George Patton

(553) Signed certificate from Mussolini himself

(554) Use of the electoral college

(555) Prime minister after Mussolini was toppled

(556) Eleven

(557) Began around 800 to 900 B.C. and lasted about 700 years before being absorbed by the Romans.

(558) Benito Mussolini

(559) Giuseppe Mazzini (1805 - 1872)

(560) Modena

(561) Giuseppe Garibaldi (1807 - 1882)

(562) Crown and Coat of Arms

(563) Rome (Treaty of Rome)

(564) Tuscany

(565) Camillo Cavour, Giuseppe Garibaldi, and Giuseppe Mazzini

(566) Name given to the northern part of Italy still controlled by Mussolini after Italy's surrender in World War II.

(567) Palatine Hill

(568) Aurora

(569) 1978

(570) Succession from Italy to establish the "Northern Republic of Padania"

(571) Julius Caesar

(572) To make the year he became prime minister, 1922, year one

(573) Military alliance between Italy and Germany

(574) Sforza

(575) 1946

(576) March 17, 1861

(577) Diocletian

(578) Lucius Junius Brutus

(579) Four popes and two queens (of France)

(580) Brought back to Milan and hung upside-down in the Piazzale Loreto

(581) Divorce

(582) Rome

(583) Spartacus

(584) Initially established in 1921

(585) 1871

(586) Unification of Italy

(587) Byzantine Empire

(588) Risorgimento

(589) Direct male descendants of the last king of Italy, Umberto II

(590) Pantone colors of the Italian flag

(591) China

(592) Giuseppe Mazzini (1805 - 1872)

(593) Redshirts

(594) Commander of the Order of Merit of the Republic of Italy

(595) Titus

(596) 1870

(597) Chamber of Deputies and Senate

Chapter 7: *Italian Americans & Immigration*

---

(598) Oldest Italian American organization in the United States

(599) Joe Pesci

(600) Eddi Arcaro (1916 - 1997)

(601) Al Capone, born Alphonso Caponi (1895 - 1947)

(602) John Alfred de Simone

(603) 90%

(604) John Francis Bongiovi

(605) Nicholas Cage

(606) 12%

(607) Francesco Vigo

(608) New York City, with approximately two million

(609) Feast of San Gennaro

(610) Cough drop

(611) Abraham Lincoln

(612) Florence. At last count, there were over twenty cities named Florence with eighteen named for

Venice and twelve named for Genoa.

(613) Massachusetts Institute of Technology

(614) He was the first enlisted man to win the Congressional Medal of Honor in World War II for his heroism at the Battle of Guadalcanal where he single-handedly killed 38 Japanese soldiers. For his bravery at the Battle of Iwo Jima, he was awarded the Navy Cross posthumously as he was killed in the battle by an exploding shell.

(615) Mr. Coffee

(616) Danny DeVito

(617) Dean Martin

(618) Lyle Alzado

(619) Frank Sinatra (1915- 1998)

(620) Marilyn Monroe

(621) Monticello

(622) Carmine Coppola and Francis Ford Coppola

(623) New Mexico

(624) Miss Liberty one dollar silver coin

(625) Most world heritage sites

(626) Marconi Wireless Company of America

(627) Rocky Marciano

(628) Rachael Ray

(629) Tim McGraw

(630) Ray Liotta

(631) Italian American Jim Gentile

(632) Polish

(633) For shooting down over 30 Nazi planes during 1944, making him the highest scoring fighter pilot in United States History and giving him the title "Ace of Aces".

(634) That he received them from shrapnel wounds suffered while fighting in France during World War I

(635) The four women Frank Sinatra was married to during his life

(636) Colorado

(637) Franco Harris

(638) Sicily

(639) Saint Louis, Missouri

(640) 95%

(641) Fred De Luca founded Subway and Anthony Conza founded Blimpie

(642) Richard Grasso, born in Queens

(643) *Journal of the American Medical Association*

(644) Harry Carry

(645) *L'Eco d'Italia*

(646) Alyssa Milano

(647) Martin Scorsese (1942 - present)

(648) Susan Sarandon, born Susan Abigail Tomalin

(649) National Italian American Foundation (www.niaf.org)

(650) Billy Martin, born Alfred Manuel Pesano

(651) Father Charles Constantine Pise

(652) Anthony Celebrezze, appointed in 1962

(653) (c) horse racing

(654) Bank of America

(655) Venice

(656) American War of Independence

(657) Tony Danza

(658) (b) *Bonanza*

(659) First Italian American professional baseball player

(660) *Fra Noi*, one of my favorites

(661) Pope Pius IX

(662) Stephen Segal

(663) Original Dixieland Jazz Band

(664) Joe Montana

(665) Geraldine Ferraro

(666) Anne Bancroft

(667) (c) Admiral

(668) 24-second shot clock

(669) Mine for gold

(670) He was the very first person of Italian heritage to hold public office. He was responsible for the defense for the English Colony of Maryland.

(671) New York, Philadelphia, Chicago, Boston and Pittsburgh - in that order

(672) One-handed lay-up

(673) Mulberry Street

(674) Giuseppe Garibaldi

(675) Vince DiMaggio, who played for the Pittsburgh Pirates, and Dom DiMaggio, who led the American League in stolen bases in 1950.

(676) *Italian-American Digest*

(677) Vincent Impellitteri

(678) Mario Lanza

(679) Ella Tambussi Grasso (1919 - 1981)

(680) Naples Street

(681) 1907

(682) Marlon Brando

(683) Rod Marinelli, replaced Steve Mariucci

(684) Peter Lemengello

(685) Employment

(686) 3,845 immigrants

(687) Walden Robert Cassotto

(688) Joann Falletta

(689) U.S. capitol, Washington, D.C.

(690) *L'Italo-Americano*

(691) Vic Damone

(692) Jeno Paulucci

(693) October

(694) Bruce Springsteen

(695) 22 year old Garrick Ohlsson

(696) Tax evasion

(697) Our Lady of the Assumption

(698) Discovering gold in Alaska in 1902 and the subsequent founding of Fairbanks

(699) Detroit, Michigan

(700) Published around the beginning of the 20th century, they were weekly Italian newspapers in America

(701) Mary Lou Retton, born Mary Lou Rettoni

(702) (a) San Francisco, on October 12th

(703) Professional wrestler

(704) *Italian Tribune*

(705) Ernest Borgnine

(706) Cindy Lauper

(707) Jay Leno

(708) Sonny Bono (1935 - 1998)

(709) Radio Flyer

(710) A 56 game hitting streak set in 1941. However, few people know that his hitting streak continued for 16 games into the following season. Thus, his combined-season hitting streak was 72 games.

(711) (a) Miss America

(712) Watergate

(713) New Castle

(714) 1 million

(715) Names for three of the first five warships commissioned by the United States Navy.

(716) Mental retardation center

(717) (a) wrestling

(718) New York City

(719) Jennifer Caprioti, born 1976

(720) United States hockey team

(721) North Dakota

(722) Barnes & Noble

(723) Blessed Virgin Mary (Our Lady of Trapani)

(724) Frank Sinatra and Dean Martin

(725) Francis Spinola

(726) Angelo Bertelli

(727) Christopher Columbus

(728) Dan Marino

(729) Symbol of the ancient Roman Republic

(730) Sally Beauty

(731) Naples

(732) Saint Cecelia of Rome

(733) John Travolta

(734) Both were members of the American Continental Congress that signed the *Declaration of Independence*

(735) Bataan Death March

(736) Tony Bennett, who took Bob Hope's advice and changed his name

(737) Mario Puzo

(738) Maria Bartiromo

(739) Alcatraz in San Francisco

(740) Francis Ford Coppola (1939 - present)

(741) San Francisco and Los Angeles

(742) *E.T.*

(743) Buffalo

(744) Costantino Brumidi (1805 - 1880)

(745) Di Giorgio

(746) Brian De Palma

(747) Syracuse University

(748) Chef Boyardee

(749) Fiorello Henry LaGuardia (1882 - 1947), son of immigrants of Italian and Jewish ancestry, was the first New York City mayor of Italian ancestry (99th mayor in total). He was elected in 1933.

(750) Nuremberg War Crimes Tribunal

(751) He overheard the melody in an Italian love song while in Sicily

(752) "All men are by nature equally free and independent". Friend Thomas Jefferson modified this phrase to become "All men are created equal".

(753) *The Italian Tribune*, published by Marlene Baker

(754) Verrazano Bridge

(755) L'Isola Della Lacrime, or Isle of Tears

(756) Rick Santelli

(757) Robert De Niro (1943 - present)

(758) World War II

(759) Tommy Lasorda

(760) Alan Alda, born 1936

(761) Order Sons of Italy in America (O.S.I.A.)

(762) Bloomfield

(763) *Apotheosis of Washington*

(764) (c) 1792, celebrating the 300th anniversary

(765) San Francisco Italian Athletic Club

(766) Sbarro

(767) Frank D. Stella

(768) *Buck Rogers*

(769) Al Pacino, born Alfredo James Pacino

(770) *Scent of a Woman*

(771) Connecticut and Rhode Island, both at 19% of their total state populations

(772) Federal Bureau of Investigation, or FBI

(773) Gonzaga University

(774) Ernest and Julio Gallo

(775) Lincoln Memorial

(776) Barber

(777) HIV, the AIDES virus

(778) Giuseppe Verdi

(779) North End

(780) Army chief of staff

(781) Alfred E. Smith, the grandson of an Italian immigrant. He lost to Herbert Hoover in 1928.

(782) Nearly 90%, with 25% from Sicily alone

(783) Cantoro's Italian Market

(784) Vince Lombardi

(785) Both won the Heisman Trophy, college football's highest award, while attending the University of Miami

(786) Apollo Space Program

(787) 14 received the medal during World War II, 10 during the Vietnam War and 6 during the U.S. Civil War.

(788) United States capitol building in Washington, D.C.

(789) "Little Italy", New York

(790) 1892

(791) "Rosie the Riveter"

(792) Enrico Fermi

(793) "Project Manhattan"

(794) Italian Stallion

(795) Senator John Ensign

(796) Hang glider

(797) American bald eagle

(798) Gary Sinise

(799) University of Michigan

(800) Joe DiMaggio (1914 - 1999)

(801) Robert De Niro

(802) The Hill

(803) New York Yankees

(804) College of William and Mary

(805) Joe Paterno

(806) Tropicana Juice Company

(807) Charles Atlas (1892-1972)

(808) Fifth, behind German, Irish, English and African

(809) *The Caddy*

(810) Senator Richard Santorum

(811) "Without Official Papers". Many Italians entering the U.S. arrived this way.

(812) *Patton*

(813) Rick Pitino

(814) *Christ in Concrete*

(815) 6 in the Senate and 23 in the House of Representatives

(816) South Philly

(817) Connie Francis

(818) Antonin Scalia, the son of Sicilian parents

(819) National Italian American Sports Hall of Fame

(820) Frankie Lane

(821) Little Italy

(822) Thomas Jefferson and Benjamin Franklin

(823) Senator Pete Domenici

(824) Fewer than 5,000

(825) United States House of Representatives

(826) (c) Augusta, Georgia

(827) Penny Marshall

(828) Rene Russo

(829) Rollie Fingers

(830) Charles "Lucky" Luciano (1897 - 1962)

(831) New York City, specifically Staten Island

(832) Church of San Carlo al Corso

(833) More than two million

(834) Guy Lombardo

(835) American Civil War, for the Union

(836) Columbus Chapel in Boalsburg, Pennsylvania

(837) Second Monday in October

(838) Syracuse

(839) Donald Duck, Woody Woodpecker and Casper the Friendly Ghost

(840) Waldensians - Italian Protestants seeking refuge

(841) Liberace

(842) *Spanish Eyes*

(843) *I'll Never Smile Again*

(844) Nick Bolletieri Tennis Academy, founded in 1976

(845) Robert Venturi

(846) Baltimore

(847) (d) $61,300

(848) Quentin Tarantino

(849) *The Right Stuff*

(850) Rear Admiral Bancroft Gherardi

(851) "Out of Many, One"

(852) Mardi Gras

(853) (c) billiards

(854) First ethnic Italian parish in America

(855) Robert Mondavi

(856) Rome, Georgia is built atop seven hills, much like Rome, Italy

(857) Judy Garland

(858) DeBartolo

(859) *National Enquirer*

(860) Frank Capra (1897 - 1991)

(861) Constantino Beltrami (1179 - 1885)

(862) *Moonstruck*

(863) Walk of Fame

(864) Yogi Berra

(865) McDonald's Big Mac

(866) Vincent Gardenia

(867) She felt a kick while viewing a Leonardo da Vinci painting in the Uffizi museum in Florence.

(868) New York

(869) 26 million

(870) Alicia Keys

(871) A.P. Giannini (1870 - 1949)

(872) 1,500

(873) Don Ameche, born Dominic Felix Amici

(874) Manager of the Year

(875) 13 received the Congressional Medal of Honor while 10 received the Navy Cross

(876) Lee Iacocca, born Lido Iacocca

(877) Mother Frances Xavier Cabrini (1850 - 1917)

(878) Fairleigh Dickinson

(879) World War II, Italy declared war on the United States after the Battle of Pearl Harbor

(880) Joe Barbera, of Hanna-Barbera Productions

(881) Christopher Columbus, on the 400th anniversary of his first voyage of discovery

(882) Yep, *Titanic*

(883) Billy the Kid

(884) Rocky Marciano

(885) Dean Martin

(886) Henry Fonda

(887) Father Francesco Bressani

(888) Garibaldi Guard

(889) Rocky Marciano

(890) Ralph Macchio

(891) Boxing

(892) Rudolph Giuliani (1944 - present)

(893) Madonna Louise Veronica Ciccone

(894) Detroit, by Alfonso Tonti. Toni also was the colonial governor of Detroit for 12 years.

(895) Sicily

(896) Santa Clara University

(897) Hoboken Four

(898) Swimming

(899) Malaria

(900) Federal Hill

(901) Samuel Alito

(902) Yogi Berra, longtime catcher for the New York Yankees

Chapter 8: *Language, Literature, & Philosophy*

(903) Solo

(904) Arena

(905) Influenza

(906) Dante, Petrarch and Boccaccio

(907) Italkian

(908) The Sweet Life (or Beautiful Life or Good Life)

(909) Little to none. Their language is still largely undeciphered.

(910) Number one

(911) Dante Alighieri (1265 - 1321)

(912) Sicily

(913) Extravaganza

(914) Calabria and Apulia

(915) Milanese

(916) Encore, which means yet again

(917) *Cinderella*, *Sleeping Beauty*, *Pinocchio*, *Rapunzel*, *Snow White*, and *Red Riding Hood*

(918) What is far from the eyes is far from the heart.

(919) Umbrella

(920) Nearly 60%. In Europe, only the Irish and British have higher percentages of people speaking only their native language.

(921) 80%

(922) Magna Charta

(923) Literature with five

(924) Giorgio Vascari (1511 - 1574)

(925) Studio

(926) Literature

(927) Cassa

(928) *The Comedy*. Divine was added during the 16th century.

(929) Address for the fictitious palace (with balcony) from Shakespeare's story *Romeo and Juliet*, the story of two lovers from the rival families of Capulet (Capelletti) and Montague (Montecchi).

(930) Florence

(931) Spanish, French, Portuguese, Rumanian and Italian, considered the most difficult to master

(932) Alibi

(933) Semper fidelis (always beautiful)

(934) Volcano

(935) Video

(936) Paste

(937) Miracle

(938) Per capita

(939) Scenario

(940) Dante Alighieri (1265 - 1321)

(941) *Il Promessi Sposi* (*The Betrothed*)

(942) A church

(943) i.e. means "that is" while e.g. means "for example"

(944) Replica

(945) No. Until a century ago, ciao was spoken only in northern Italy and was considered formal usage.

(946) A seaview

(947) Presepio

(948) Twice a day

(949) Fiasco

(950) Let the buyer beware

(951) A cat

(952) Love thy neighbor as thyself

(953) Roman names for the days of the week

(954) Watermark

(955) The End

(956) Black Death

(957) The family is sacred

(958) Caesar

(959) Mural

(960) Galileo Galilei

(961) 19th century. English officially replaced Latin in 1847.

(962) Italo Calvino (1923 - 1985)

(963) Syracuse in Sicily. However, this city was a Greek colony during Plato's time.

(964) To say "You're welcome"

(965) Lava

(966) Vacations many Italians take during August

(967) Tuscan Italian

(968) Hebrew

(969) Stucco

(970) Men from the northern part of Italy typically end this name with the letter "O", while men from southern Italy typically end this name with the letter "A".

(971) "Fine view" or "beautiful view"

(972) Get your attention

(973) Ancient language spoken by some decedents of Albanians

(974) American Revolution. His book was titled *A History of the War of Independence*.

(975) Commando

(976) Graffiti

(977) *Il Principe* (*The Prince*)

(978) Julius Caesar

(979) Confetti

(980) "From the founding of the city (Rome)"

(981) Infantry, meaning foot soldiers

(982) *The Lives of the Most Eminent Painters, Sculptors and Architects*

(983) Contraband

(984) Sardinian

(985) Politically cunning

(986) Little book

(987) 50 B.C.

(988) I came, I saw, I conquered

(989) Motto

(990) Vandalism

(991) Auguri

(992) Romance languages

(993) Heaven, Hell (inferno) and Purgatory

(994) Atrium

(995) Ghetto

(996) Alessandro Manzoni (1785 - 1873)

(997) Greek

(998) "Our Sea"

(999) Arrivederci is the familiar form & arrivederLa is the formal form

(1000) Finale

(1001) Not to be confused with the word stink in English, stinco means shinbone in Italian.

(1002) Giovanni Boccaccio (1313 - 1375)

(1003) Semicentennial and Centennial, respectively

Chapter 9: *Military History & Contributions*

(1004) Attila the Hun

(1005) Condottieri

(1006) Erwin Rommel

(1007) Hannibal

(1008) Fascist Ten Commandments

(1009) Marc Antony and Cleopatra

(1010) Cicero

(1011) Malta

(1012) Only one, the Roma. This ship was sunk by a German missile to ensure the ship did not fall into Allied control after Italy surrendered and subsequently declared war on Germany.

(1013) Approximately 20%

(1014) Masada

(1015) Military words with origins in the Italian language

(1016) Fewer than 15,000

(1017) Sicily

(1018) Scipio (the Elder) Africanus

(1019) Period of peace and advancement in the ancient Roman Empire.

(1020) Praetorian Guard

(1021) Zero. Italy was constructing the first of three planned aircraft carriers; however, they scuttled the unfinished ship to prevent it from falling into German hands.

(1022) Soviet Union

(1023) Cleopatra

(1024) Raised arm, similar to the ancient Roman salute

(1025) France and Great Britain

(1026) Scotland

(1027) Venice

(1028) Germany, where the Luftwaffe (air force) carried out Blitzkriegs

(1029) French General Napoleon Bonaparte

(1030) Carthage

(1031) Submarine

(1032) Pantelleria

(1033) Cassino

(1034) Cannons

(1035) 475 years, ending in 420 A.D.

(1036) Bombarda

(1037) Normans

(1038) Le Folgore

(1039) Educated Greeks

(1040) Partisans, or rebel fighters, fighting the Fascist regime

(1041) Celts

(1042) January 1, 2005

(1043) World War I

(1044) Transmit Fascist propaganda to Arabic nations to gain their allegiance.

(1045) War Galley

(1046) Held captive as a prisoner of war

(1047) Sicily

(1048) Germany

(1049) Only Roman citizens could be legionnaires, while auxiliaries were noncitizens and aides to legionnaires.

(1050) Attila the Hun

(1051) Salve for wounds

(1052) Ponte Vecchio

(1053) Sword, dagger and javelin

(1054) From wounds received during fighting in World War I

(1055) Colonel from colonnello, corporal from capo and captain.

(1056) Piloted a captured American P-38 to disguise himself as an Allied fighter escort

(1057) Hadrian's Wall, located in northern England

(1058) Ethiopia

(1059) French

(1060) Between 25 and 33, depending on the decree of the emperor

(1061) From the area immediately encircling the emperor's tent, called the Praetorium

(1062) Four - Roma, Impero, Vittorio Veneto, and Littorio (later renamed Italia)

(1063) (c) 600 years

(1064) Elephants

(1065) Germany, via the Berlin-Rome Axis treaty

(1066) Silver eagle

(1067) Rome was sacked and ravaged by the Vandals, a Germanic tribe

(1068) Aircraft carrier

(1069) Etruscans

(1070) 500,000

> **Chapter 10:** *Music, Art, & Architecture*

(1071) *The Last Supper*

(1072) Vatican library

(1073) Aqueduct

(1074) Canada

(1075) Gioacchino Rossini (1792 - 1868) with his William Tell Overture

(1076) Federico Fellini (1920 - 1993)

(1077) Architecture

(1078) Spain, as in the Spanish Steps

(1079) Norman dello Joio

(1080) Giacomo Puccini

(1081) Antonio Stradivari (1644 - 1737).

(1082) Filippo Brunelleschi (1377 - 1446)

(1083) Approximately 615 (45 operas, 70 sonatas and about 500 concertos)

(1084) Frederic Bartholdi

(1085) Estimated at 1,200,000,000

(1086) Mother of French-born Italian Frederic Auguste Bertholdi, the creator of the statue

(1087) Recently won by Laura Pausini

(1088) Official residences of the Roman emperors for over 300 years

(1089) 1908

(1090) Venice

(1091) French

(1092) Roman Colosseum

(1093) Looting of the King Herod the Great Temple in Jerusalem, which occurred about A.D. 70.

(1094) 16th century Florence

(1095) Christmas

(1096) Jewish

(1097) Rudolph Valentino (1895 - 1926)

(1098) Hermitage and Royal Palace

(1099) Saint Peter's Basilica

(1100) Constant vibration of the city's heavy traffic

(1101) Import, export and transfer of cultural property, such as ancient Roman artifacts.

(1102) Andrea Palladio (1518 - 1580)

(1103) Approximately 1400 to 1600 A.D.

(1104) Leonardo da Vinci

(1105) El Escorial, both a museum and royal palace

(1106) Experiencing Carnevale during a visit to Rome

(1107) 1173 A.D.

(1108) Aqua Appia

(1109) Arturo Toscanini (1867 - 1957)

(1110) Michelangelo's

(1111) Vincenzo Bellini

(1112) Anna Maria Alberghetti

(1113) Pantheon

(1114) Michelangelo

(1115) Sandro Botticelli (1445 - 1510)

(1116) (c) 60%

(1117) He played Rodolfo in *La Boheme*

(1118) *La Pieta*

(1119) Venice

(1120) About 12,000

(1121) Luigi Pirandello

(1122) Sister of the famous Italian explorer Amerigo Vespucci

(1123) *School of Athens*

(1124) Female opera singer

(1125) Salvatore Cammanaro

(1126) Antonio Vivaldi (1678 - 1741)

(1127) Green (marble from Prato), white (marble from Carrara), and red (marble from Moremma)

(1128) Ballerina

(1129) La Scala was built on the site of an old church called Santa Maria della Scala, or Saint Mary of the Stairs.

(1130) Guy Lombardo with his Royal Canadian orchestra

(1131) Florence, in 1915

(1132) Giovanni Pierluigi Palestrina (1526 - 1594)

(1133) Constanzi Theater

(1134) Luigi Barzini, born 1908

(1135) First motion picture with sound produced in Italy

(1136) Surprisingly none

(1137) Giorgione (1477 - 1510)

(1138) 26 (20 Grammy Awards, 2 Emmy Awards and 4 Academy Awards)

(1139) Pause between important musical pieces, an intermission

(1140) 18th century, born in 1782

(1141) Cinecitta

(1142) Licia Albanese

(1143) Venice

(1144) Oratorio

(1145) *Pieta Rondanini*

(1146) Enrico Caruso

(1147) *Fantasia*

(1148) He overheard someone remark that *La Pieta* was sculpted by another artist. In his resulting frustration, he inscribed his name to eliminate any confusion.

(1149) Capella

(1150) Pietro Francesco Cavalli

(1151) Zampogna

(1152) Three years, from 1503 to 1506

(1153) Florence, near the Palazzo Vecchio

(1154) Dante Alighieri (1265 - 1321)

(1155) Claudio Monteverdi (1567 - 1643)

(1156) Andrea Bocelli (1958 - present)

(1157) Cimabue, born Bencivieni di Pepo (1240 - 1302)

(1158) Louvre, located in Paris

(1159) Andrea Bocelli (1958 - present)

(1160) A comet. Thought to be Halley's Comet.

(1161) *Norma*

(1162) Buonarroti

(1163) Venice

(1164) Powdered pigment mixed only with water

(1165) Spaghetti Westerns

(1166) Giotto di Bondone (1267 - 1337)

(1167) (c) Masaccio

(1168) (b) central Italy

(1169) Palazzo Nuovo and the Palazzo dei Conservatori

(1170) Blessed Virgin Mary

(1171) Violin

(1172) Maestro

(1173) Sergio Leone

(1174) Raphael, Raffaello Sanzio da Urbino (1483 - 1520)

(1175) Naples

(1176) Gasparo Bertolotti

(1177) Keyboard

(1178) Rekindle Greek music and drama

(1179) *Breakfast at Tiffany's* and *The Pink Panther*

(1180) New York Stock Exchange and United States Supreme Court

(1181) Oil painting

(1182) Hadrian

(1183) 19th century Japan

(1184) Unset lime plaster

(1185) Harry Warren

(1186) Arc de Triomphe

(1187) *Falstaff*

(1188) Opera

(1189) Michelangelo Buonarroti (1475 - 1564)

(1190) To the Virgin Mary

(1191) Titian, born Tiziano Vecellio

(1192) Dante Alighieri (1265 - 1321)

(1193) Modern-day Tunisia. Running 87 miles, this aqueduct was built in the 2nd century A.D. to supply Carthage.

(1194) Leonardo da Vinci

(1195) Santa Croce

(1196) *Euridice*

(1197) Rome

(1198) In the third person as "the voice"

(1199) Emperor Vespasian, but not completely finished until the time of his sons Titus and Domitian.

(1200) Teatro Dell'Opera

(1201) Frank Signorelli

(1202) Norman dello Joio

(1203) Sicily

(1204) Paparazzi

(1205) Vincent Rose

(1206) Church of Santa Croce in Florence, Tuscany

Chapter 11: Sciences, Biology, & Invention

(1207) Mathematics

(1208) (a) University of Pisa

(1209) Medical thermometer

(1210) Gabriel Fallopius (1523 - 1562)

(1211) Galileo Galilei

(1212) First national park in the world

(1213) First commercial liens

(1214) Liguria, due to its mild winters

(1215) Absolute differential calculus

(1216) Camillo Golgi (1843 - 1926)

(1217) Rapier

(1218) 220 volts

(1219) Fractional line, such as 1/4 or 1/2

(1220) Bridge which allowed strings of a violin to be raised off the instrument to greatly enhance sound.

(1221) Discovery of the first asteroid

(1222) First citizen of Italy to travel to Space

(1223) Premature heart attack

(1224) Giovanni Battista Belzoni

(1225) Purified crystal glass

(1226) Guglielmo Marconi (1874 - 1937)

(1227) Roma

(1228) Ballet

(1229) Probability, as in Father of Probability

(1230) Salerno (Sicily), at the University of Salerno

(1231) Neck ties and socks. Socks, or hosa as they were called by the Romans, were said to be introduced by Julius Caesar.

(1232) Ageing

(1233) Hydrofoil

(1234) University of Bologna

(1235) Paris, France

(1236) Music

(1237) Horseshoes

(1238) Flora

(1239) Shoes crafted with one designed for the right foot and one designed for the left foot

(1240) Speed of sound. The modern and refined measurement for the speed of sound is 1,087 feet per second, darn close.

(1241) Crossword puzzles

(1242) Enrico Fermi (1901 - 1954)

(1243) Colorless glass

(1244) Cello

(1245) Glass cups and vessels

(1246) Julius Caesar (102 B.C. - 44 B.C.)

(1247) Pants or trousers

(1248) BBC, or the British Broadcasting Corporation

(1249) Geologically speaking, Italy is rather young. As a result, fossil fuels and minerals have not had enough time to develop.

(1250) Employing special holograms impressed on the wine cap

(1251) Encyclopedias, a crude version was developed by the ancient Romans during the 1st century B.C.

(1252) Galileo Galilei

(1253) Great Wall of China

(1254) (a) Rome, around 380 A.D.

(1255) First recorded official orphanage

(1256) For his invention of the radio that enabled the passengers to call for help. This call was answered by the nearby ship Carpathia.

(1257) Milan

(1258) Discovered Mercury and Venus and measured their rotations

(1259) Do-re-mi-fa-sol-la-te-do

(1260) Eight-track tape player

(1261) Seismograph

(1262) Venice. They are boat ambulances.

(1263) Glass windows

(1264) Illuminous material. Once heated by the sun, this material would glow in the dark for an extended period of time.

(1265) Fiction

(1266) Gregorian chant

(1267) Face cards - king, queen and jack

(1268) Handkerchief

(1269) Wireless radio

(1270) 113 for general emergencies, 112 for police emergencies, 115 for fire emergencies and 118 for medical emergencies.

(1271) Coin toss

(1272) Rocket-propelled flight-ejection system (ejection seat). He also enhanced his invention with the first automatic parachute deployment system with a break-away glass canopy.

(1273) Concrete

(1274) Presto (very fast), allegro (fast), and andante (medium)

(1275) Corrective spectacles (eyeglasses)

(1276) (c) fourth

(1277) Enrico Fermi, an Italian Jew

(1278) Year of Our Lord

(1279) Messina

(1280) Fiberglass

(1281) 4,800 feet, or one thousand paces

(1282) Invented around 50 B.C. by the Romans

(1283) Venice

(1284) Florence

(1285) %, percentage sign

(1286) Bari

(1287) Galileo Galilei

(1288) World's first central heating system. Typically consisted of a wood or coal burning furnace located in the basement where heat was then distributed to the villa above.

(1289) To tell time. The Roman clepsydra was a water clock.

(1290) "E pur si muove" ("And yet it moves" - the earth around the sun)

(1291) Pentagram

(1292) Flute

(1293) Salvador Luria

(1294) Ring around the rosies; A pocket full of posies; Ashes, Ashes; We all fall down!

(1295) Lighthouse

(1296) Candles. These candles were even eaten when food was scarce.

(1297) First recorded maps

(1298) Alessandro Volta (1745 - 1827). The electrical Volt is fittingly named for him.

(1299) Political cartoons

(1300) Set and harden underwater

(1301) Telephone. Antonio Meucci also invented the smokeless candle.

(1302) Galileo Galilei

(1303) Black Death killed about a third of Italy's 10 million people from A.D. 1347 to 1351.

(1304) W and Z field particles, or subatomic particles

(1305) Diamond

(1306) University of Padua

(1307) First V engine, V12 engine and independent front suspension

(1308) Florence

(1309) Padova

(1310) Stone mile markers placed at intervals of 1,000 paces apart, a Roman mile

(1311) A harpsichord that can play both soft and loud (piano for soft and forte for loud)

(1312) Cryptology

(1313) Stradivari's Alard violin of 1715

(1314) Venice

(1315) Argentina

(1316) Genoa

(1317) Sewer system

(1318) Written musical notation

(1319) Pi

(1320) Giotto di Bondone (1266 - 1337)

(1321) Julian calendar. He replaced the flawed ten month calendar with a twelve month calendar that included leap years.

(1322) Venice

(1323) Life insurance

(1324) Venice

(1325) 400. D is 500 and C is 100, thus 500-100=400

(1326) Military battlefield hospital

(1327) Salerno School of Medicine

(1328) Leonardo Fibonacci or Leonard of Pisa (1180 - 1250)

(1329) Trade unions or guilds. The first trade unions were for shoemakers, barbers and others in the craft trade.

(1330) Venice

(1331) Typewriter

(1332) Ballista

(1333) July for Julius Caesar and August for his nephew and first emperor of Rome, Augustus. Prior to the change, July was known as Quintilis.

(1334) Tartaglia (aka Noccolo Fontana)

(1335) Belgium

(1336) Florence

(1337) Fax machine

(1338) Albano

(1339) Jacuzzi

(1340) 260

(1341) Magenta, once an important silk town.

(1342) First battery

(1343) Condom

(1344) First public physicians, originating during the Middle Ages

(1345) Cologne

(1346) Sign language

(1347) Galileo Galilei

(1348) Evangelista Torricelli (1608 - 1647). His is also known for developing what is known as Torricelli's Theorem, relating to calculus.

(1349) Nitroglycerine

(1350) Pinocchio

(1351) Patents

(1352) Written perfectly backward

(1353) The $\sum$ letter, or membership sign

(1354) Syringe

(1355) Bartolommeo Cristofori (1655 - 1731)

(1356) Compass

(1357) Leonardo da Vinci

(1358) Felice Matteucci and Eugenio Barsanti, a priest

Chapter 12: *Sports, Leisure, & Fashion*

(1359) Four, with six appearances in the championship game

(1360) 15 for individual bocce and 18 for team bocce

(1361) Ludovico Ariosto

(1362) Middle Ages

(1363) *Blood and Sand*

(1364) Nearly 9,000

(1365) Bocce

(1366) La Regatta

(1367) "Garbo", which is a general reference for styles or clothes

(1368) Circus

(1369) Mario Andretti

(1370) Toga

(1371) Giuseppe Verdi (1813 - 1901)

(1372) Sophia Loren (1934 - present)

(1373) Calcio

(1374) Fur coat worn in Sardinia

(1375) Gabriela Sabatini

(1376) Raga

(1377) (b) 1976

(1378) *Yes, Giorgio*

(1379) Basketball

(1380) George Di Centa

(1381) Guccio Gucci

(1382) Sofia Scicolone

(1383) Benito Mussolini. She was once married to Romano Mussolini

(1384) Milan

(1385) Holland

(1386) Day accommodations only - typically consisting of a bathroom, shower and other cleaning facilities for a traveler.

(1387) Medicine

(1388) Greece

(1389) One or two star hotel

(1390) Giorgio Armani

(1391) Bowling

(1392) Joe Torre

(1393) Bingo

(1394) Villa rustica

(1395) $15 billion

(1396) Lombardi Trophy

(1397) Soccer

(1398) Professional hockey in the National Hockey League (NHL)

(1399) Gianni Versace

(1400) *James Bond* movies

(1401) Roberto Baggio

(1402) Eleanora Duse (1859 - 1924)

(1403) December 1, 1970

(1404) 55,000

(1405) Montana, Italy (now a town in neighboring Slovenia)

(1406) Milan

Chapter 13: *Travel, Destinations, & Geography*

(1407) Valle d'Aosta

(1408) L'Aquila

(1409) Northern most major town in Italy, borders Austria

(1410) Cumae

(1411) 600 tons of lead

(1412) Medici

(1413) Venice, on the island of Torcello

(1414) Piazza

(1415) The Seven Hills of Rome

(1416) South of Cortona in Umbria

(1417) Ravenna

(1418) France, Spain and the United States - in that order.

(1419) Trentino-Alto Adige, previously part of the Austrian-Hungarian Empire

(1420) Torre di Pisa (Leaning Tower of Pisa)

(1421) Rome

(1422) San Marino

(1423) Casa Guidi

(1424) Castel del Monte

(1425) Mount Vesuvius

(1426) Assisi

(1427) Aosta

(1428) Fiesole

(1429) Corsica

(1430) Sicily and Calabria. The provinces of Messina and Reggio di Calabria were devastated.

(1431) Milan

(1432) Venice

(1433) Roman Forum

(1434) Gran Sasso and Mountain of Laga

(1435) San Marino, the world's oldest and smallest republic

(1436) Le Marches and Emilia-Romagna

(1437) Switzerland and France

(1438) Ponte Rialto

(1439) Magna Graecia (Greater Greece)

(1440) Milan

(1441) Uffizi

(1442) From the patron saint of Venice, Saint Mark, whose own symbol was the lion.

(1443) Val Grande

(1444) Rimini

(1445) Leaning Tower of Pisa

(1446) Ostia Antica

(1447) Messina

(1448) Verona

(1449) Greater Greece

(1450) Capua

(1451) Venice

(1452) Marches

(1453) Founded on the Palatine Hill, or Collis Palatinus in Latin, with the capital on capitaline Hill.

(1454) Italy's natural beauty

(1455) Trieste

(1456) Agrigento

(1457) Venice

(1458) France, Switzerland, Austria, Slovenia, San Marino, and Vatican City

(1459) Gulf of Taranto

(1460) University of Padua

(1461) Ireland

(1462) Livorno

(1463) Sardinia, specifically the northeast coast

(1464) Piazza Armerina

(1465) Lipizzaner horses

(1466) Friuli-Venezia Giulia, Valle d'Aosta, Calabria, Sicily and Sardinia

(1467) Siena

(1468) Tiber

(1469) Florence

(1470) Isle of Elba

(1471) Po valley

(1472) Verona

(1473) La Scala

(1474) Sardinia

(1475) Tivoli

(1476) Amalfi Drive, which runs between Naples and Sorrento

(1477) Po

(1478) Bay of Naples

(1479) Mangia Tower

(1480) Siracusa

(1481) Ravenna

(1482) Herculaneum. Resina now sits atop the buried town.

(1483) Approximately 10%

(1484) Lombardy, named for the Lombards or "long beards"

(1485) Mount Vesuvius, in 1944

(1486) Sanremo

(1487) Sicily and Sardinia

(1488) San Reno

(1489) Mont Blanc (Monte Bianco) at 4,810 meters and located in Valle d'Aosta

(1490) Via dei Tornabuoni

(1491) Palermo

(1492) Mountain chain in northern Italy primarily spanning the Trentino-Alto Adige region

(1493) Roman Colosseum

(1494) Sicily

(1495) Planned city in southern Italy by Mussolini to promote economic growth similar to that of northern Italy

(1496) Rome (Roma)

(1497) Sicily (Sicilia)

(1498) Saint Peter's Basilica

(1499) Second

(1500) On the battlefront between Albania and Greece

(1501) Milan

(1502) Largest active volcano in Europe

(1503) Rialto

(1504) Nearby swamps provided better defense than what was available in Rome

(1505) Modena

(1506) Borromean Islands

(1507) Compagnia Italiana Turismo

(1508) Grand Canal

(1509) (c) 28%

(1510) Florence (Firenze)

(1511) Syracuse (Siracusa)

(1512) Ravenna

(1513) Portofino

(1514) Arizona, but with over ten times more people

(1515) Lucca

(1516) Santa Maria del Fiore

(1517) Corsica

(1518) Arezzo

(1519) Lombardy

(1520) Naples

(1521) Cagliari

(1522) 2,000 of the 20,000 residents

(1523) Campania

(1524) Saint Peter, one of Christ's twelve apostles and the first pope

(1525) Elba, located in Tuscany

(1526) Loreto

(1527) Venice

(1528) Gaeta, near Naples

(1529) London

(1530) "New City"

(1531) Arno

(1532) Bari, capital of Apulia

(1533) Vatican City

(1534) Orvieto

(1535) Straight of Messina (Streeto di Messina)

(1536) Lake Como

(1537) Four - Rome, Milan, Naples and Turin

(1538) Amalfi

(1539) Cremona

(1540) Frascati

(1541) Twenty

(1542) Julius Caesar, Romeo & Juliet, The Merchant of Vino, Othello and The Taming of the Shrew

(1543) Apulia

(1544) Boboli Gardens

(1545) Venice

(1546) Lazio and Emilia-Romagna

(1547) Liguria

(1548) Genoa

(1549) Siena

(1550) Apennine

(1551) Horserace turn post

(1552) Monaco

(1553) Slovenia

(1554) Saint Mark's campanile

(1555) Turin (Torino)

(1556) 1,500

(1557) Home to the butchers of Florence

(1558) Cortona

(1559) Lake Garda

(1560) Messina

(1561) Bologna

(1562) San Gimignano

(1563) Tuscany

(1564) Pisa

(1565) Parma

(1566) Austrian-Hungarian Empire, relinquished control after defeat in the war

(1567) Taranto

(1568) Imperia

(1569) Destined to flourish

(1570) Sardinia and Corsica

(1571) Naples

(1572) Torcello

(1573) Cerveteri

(1574) Venice

(1575) "Spur" of the boot

(1576) Carrara

(1577) Bologna

(1578) Genoa

(1579) Marche (Marches)

(1580) Cologne

(1581) Southern Italy spanning Calabria and Basilicata

(1582) Florence

(1583) Budapest

(1584) Murano (Vetri Murano glass)

(1585) Trentino-Alto Adige, Friuli-Venezia Giulia, Sardinia, Sicily and Valle d' Aosta

(1586) Marche (Marches)

(1587) Palermo

(1588) Genoa

(1589) Paestum

(1590) Abruzzo

(1591) Aosta Valley (Valle d'Aosta)

(1592) Apulia (Puglia)

(1593) Basilicata

(1594) Calabria

(1595) Campania

(1596) Emilia-Romagna

(1597) Friuli-Venezia Giulia

(1598) Latium (Lazio)

(1599) Liguria

(1600) Lombardy (Lombardia)

(1601) Marches (Marche)

(1602) Molise

(1603) Piedmont (Piedmonte)

(1604) Sardinia (Sardegna)

(1605) Sicily (Sicilia)

(1606) Trentino-South Tyrol (Trentino-Alto Adige)

(1607) Tuscany (Toscana)

(1608) Umbria

(1609) Veneto

Chapter 14: *World Rankings*

(1610) (c) 6th, with 5 winners. France leads with 14.

(1611) (a) 6th, producing about 15.7 million tons of fruit annually. China is tops at 77 million tons.

(1612) (a) 5th, the United States is #1

(1613) Lowest birthrate in Europe

(1614) (b) 5th, at about 330,000 tons

(1615) (c) 9th, Germany is #1

(1616) (b) 10th, with a 2005 GDP of approximately $1.65 trillion

(1617) (a) 1st, with one doctor per 165 people

(1618) (a) 3rd, with 559 police personnel per 100,000 people

(1619) (c) 3rd, at 48 liters of wine annually

(1620) (c) 5th

(1621) (b) 11th, with about 480,000 kilometers of roads

(1622) (b) 4th

(1623) (b) 15th, with about 74 vehicles per kilometer of road

(1624) (a) 22nd, with 58.8 million people in 2005

(1625) (a) 17th, with 16,300 kilometers of railway tracks. The U.S. is number one with 233,800 kilometers of railway tracks.

(1626) (b) 2nd, with a median age of 42.3 in 2005

(1627) (c) 4th, with approximately 40 million tourists annually

(1628) (c) 11th

(1629) (b) 7th, with about $2.5 billion in donated aid

(1630) (a) 6th, with $216 billion in annual manufacturing

CONCLUSION

Thank you for your interest in **Ultimate Italian Trivia**. Planning, researching and writing the trivia found in this book took a substantial amount of time and resources. I hope you enjoyed each and every trivia. As you can imagine, I am quite pleased and proud of this and my other authored books.

If you are interested in including additional trivia for the next printing and edition, I highly encourage you to contact me. Your thoughts on how well you liked my book are most appreciated. I am very much approachable. Please give me another year or so before starting a conversation with me in Italian. I'm not there yet, but will be shortly.

For those interested in learning more about the wealth management solutions offered by my company, Frush Financial Group, or my *Journal of Asset Allocation*, please do not hesitate to contact me by telephone or email. At present, I am welcoming new clients who value trusted counsel, ethical excellence, superior financial expertise, strong personal relationships, and a passionate desire to see people succeed financially, spiritually, and psychologically.

ArrivederLa,
Scott Paul Frush

CONTACT INFORMATION

Frush Financial Group
37000 Woodward Avenue, Suite 101
Bloomfield Hills, Michigan 48304

Phone: (248) 642-6800
Email: SFrush@Frush.com

INFORMATION REQUEST FORM
Frush Financial Group
- - - Investor Kit - - -

In association with TD Ameritrade Institutional

I Prefer:

☐ A brochure and application to be sent to me

☐ To be contacted by telephone

► Please send me information on the following wealth management services:

☐ Investment Management ☐ Catholic Values Investing

☐ IRA/401(k) Rollover   ☐ Trust and Estate Planning

☐ Educational/529 Savings   ☐ Money Market Accounts

☐ Certificates of Deposit   ☐ Life Insurance

☐ Tax Preparation   ☐ *Journal of Asset Allocation*

Requested information, including our ADV-II, will be mailed promptly.

► **MAIL TO:**

Name (First M. Last):_____

Street:_____

City, State Zip:_____

Telephone:_____

INFORMATION REQUEST FORM
Frush Financial Group
- - - Investor Kit - - -
In association with TD Ameritrade Institutional

You may submit this request by telephone, fax, email, or mail. Please submit your request using the contact information noted below:

▶ Mailing Address:

Frush Financial Group
37000 Woodward Avenue, Suite 101
Bloomfield Hills, MI 48304

▶ Telephone Number: (248) 642-6800

▶ Fax Number: (248) 232-1501

▶ Email: SFrush@Frush.com

APPENDIX A: ITALIAN RESOURCES

ITALIAN AMERICAN PUBLICATIONS

> ***ITALIAN TRIBUNE***
> *Marlene Baker, Publisher*
> P.O. Box 380407
> Clinton Township, MI 48038
>
> (586) 783-3260
> www.Italian-Tribune.com

> ***ITALIAN TRIBUNE***
> *A.J. Buddy Fortunato, Publisher*
> 7 North Willow Street, Suite 7
> Montclair, NJ 07042
>
> (973) 485-6000
> www.ItalianTribune.com

> ***FRA NOI***
> *Anthony J. Fornelli, Publisher*
> 3800 Division Street
> Stone Park, IL 60165
>
> (708) 338-0690
> www.FraNoi.com

> ***AMBASSADOR MAGAZINE***
> *Kevin Heitz, Senior Editor*
> 1860 19TH Street, N.W.
> Washington, DC 20009
>
> (202) 387-0600
> www.NIAF.org

> ***PRIMO MAGAZINE***
> *Truby Chiaviello, Pub. & Editor*
> 2125 Observatory Place, N.W.
> Washington, DC 20007
>
> (202) 333-0508
> www.flprimo.com

> ***ITALIAN AMERICAN***
> *Dona De Sanctis, Editor-in-Chief*
> 219 East Street, N.W.
> Washington, DC 20002
>
> (202) 547-2900
> www.OSIA.org

ITALY MAGAZINE
Middle Farm, Middle Farm Way
Poundbury, Dorchester, Dorset
United Kingdom DTI 3RS

+44 (0) 1305 266710
www.ItalyMag.co.uk

NIAF NEWS
Monica Soladay, Editor
1860 19th Street, N.W.
Washington, DC 20009

(202) 387-0600
www.NIAF.org

ITALIA!
Paul Pettengale, Editor
Suite 6, Piccadilly House
London Road, Bath BA1 6PL

+44 (0) 1225 489984
www.Italia-Magazine.com

ITALIAN AMERICANA
Carol Bonomo, Editor
80 Washington Street
Providence, RI 02903

(401) 277-5306
http://autocrat.uri.edu/1663.html.com

ITALY ITALY MAGAZINE
Italian American Multimedia Corp
P.O. Box 1255
New York, NY 10116

(800) 984-8259
www.ItalyItalyMagazine.com

AMERICAN ITALIAN HERITAGE DIGEST
Philip J. DiNovo, Editor
P.O. Box 3136
Albany, NY 12203

(518) 435-0591
www.AIHA-Albany.org

AMERICA & ITALIA REVIEW
c/o Italian American Museum
28 West 44th Street
New York, NY 10036

(212) 642-2020
www.AmericaItaliaReview.com

ITALIAN-AMERICAN DIGEST
Joseph Maselli, Publisher
P.O. Box 2392
New Orleans, LA 70176

(504) 522-7294
www.AIRF.org

L'ITALO-AMERICANO
Robert Barbera, Publisher
10631 Vinedale Street
Sun Valley, CA 91352

(818) 767-3413
www.ItaloAmericano.com

ALTRE VOCI
Italian Cultural Center
P.O. Box 189427
Sacramento, CA 95818

(916) 482-5900
www.ItalianCenter.net

LA VOCE ITALIANA
Italian Cultural & Community Ctr
1101 Milford
Houston, TX 77006

(713) 524-4222
www.HoustonItalianCenter.com

LA GAZZETTA ITALIANA
Paul Sciria, Publisher
P.O. Box 222
Hudson, OH 44236

(330) 655-7211
www.LAGazzettaItaliana.com

ITALY DOWN UNDER
478 William Street
West Melbourne
Victoria 3003, Australia

+61 (3) 9328 1433
www.ItalyDownUnder.com.au

THE ITALIC WAY
Italic Institute of America
P.O. Box 818
Floral Park, NY 11001

(516) 488-7400
www.Italic.org

AATI NEWSLETTER
Elissa Tognozzi, Editor
212 Royce Hall
Los Angeles, CA 90095

(310) 794-8910
www.AATI-Online.org

U.S. ITALIAN WEEKLY
Empire State Building
350 Fifth Avenue, 59th Floor
New York, NY 10118

(212) 601-2693
www.USItalia.info

ITALIAN CULTURE
Joseph Francese, Publisher
1405 S. Harrison Road
East Lansing, MI 48823

(517) 355-9543 ext. 130
http://msupress.msu.edu/journals/ic/

ITALIAN COOKING & LIVING
Micol Negrin,Editor
302 Fifth Avenue, 9th Floor
New York, NY 10001

(888) 742-2373
www.italiancookingandliving.com

THE ITALIAN MAGAZINE
3-4 Riverside Court
Lower Bristol Rd, Bath
BA2 3DZ, United Kingdom

+44 (0)1225 786800
Fred Dutton, Editor

POCHE PAROLE
Italian Cultural Society
4848 Battery Lane, Suite 100
Bethesda, MD 20814

(202) 333-2426
www.ItalianCulturalSociety.org

ITALIAN AMERICAN ORGANIZATIONS

NATIONAL ITALIAN AMERICAN FOUNDATION
1860 19th Street, N.W.
Washington, DC 20009

(202) 387-0600
www.NIAF.org

ORDER SONS OF ITALY IN AMERICA
219 East Street, N.W.
Washington, DC 20002

(202) 547-2900
www.OSIA.org

ITALIAN CATHOLIC FEDERATION

675 Hegenberger Road, Suite 230
Oakland, CA 94621

(510) 633-9058
www.ICF.org

THE STATUE OF LIBERTY-ELLIS ISLAND FOUNDATION

292 Madison Avenue
New York, NY 10017

(212) 561-4588
www.EllisIsland.org

UNICO NATIONAL

271 U.S. Highway West
Fairfield, NJ 07004

(973) 808-0035
www.UNICO.org

FIERI INTERNATIONAL

89-29 Shore Parkway, Unit #2
Howard Beach, NY 11414

www.Fieri.org

NATIONAL ORGANIZATION OF ITALIAN AMERICAN WOMEN

445 West 59th Street, Suite 1248
New York, NY 10019

(212) 237-8574
www.NOIAW.org

NATIONAL ITALIAN AMERICAN BAR ASSOCIATION

2020 Pennsylvania Avenue, N.W.
Washington, DC 20006

www.NIABA.org

ITALIAN AMERICAN WRITERS ASSOCIATION

P.O. Box 2011
New York, NY 10013

(212) 625-3499
www.IAWA.net

ITALIAN GENEALOGICAL GROUP

P.O. Box 626
Bethpage, NY 11714

www.Italiangen.org

ITALIAN AMERICAN MUSEUM

28 West 44th Street, 17th Floor
New York, NY 10036

(212) 642-2020
www.ItalianAmericanMuseum.org

AMERICAN-ITALIAN HERITAGE ASSOCIATION

P.O. Box 3136
Albany, NY 12203

(518) 435-0591
www.AIHA-Albany.org

ITALIA UNITA

35 Bennington Street
East Boston, MA 02128

(617) 561-3201
www.ItaliaUnita.org

AMERICAN ASSOCIATION OF TEACHERS OF ITALIAN

212 Royce Hall
Los Angeles, CA 90095

(310) 794-8910
www.AATI-Online.org

GARIBALDI MEUCCI MUSEUM

420 Tompkins Avenue Rosebank
Staten Island, NY 10305

(718) 442-1608
www.OSIA.org

THE ITALIAN HISTORICAL SOCIETY OF AMERICA

410 Park Avenue, Suite 1530
New York, NY 10022

(718) 852-2929
www.ItalianHistorical.org

THE ITALIAN CULTURAL SOCIETY OF WASHINGTON

4848 Battery Lane, Suite 100
Bethesda, MD 20814

(202) 333-2426
www.ItalianCulturalSociety.org

NATIONAL ITALIAN AMERICAN SPORTS HALL OF FAME

1431 West Taylor Street
Chicago, IL 60607

(312) 226-5566
www.NIASHF.org

ITALY AMERICA CHAMBER OF COMMERCE

730 Fifth Avenue, Suite 600
New York, NY 10019

(212) 459-0044
www.ItalChamber.org

ITALIAN AMERICAN CHAMBER OF COMMERCE

24801 Capital Boulevard
Clinton Township, MI 48036

(586) 493-4034
www.IACCM.org

ITALIAN AMERICAN CHAMBER OF COMMERCE

30 S. Michigan Avenue, Ste 504
Chicago, IL 60603

(312) 553-9137
www.ItalianChamber.us

ITALIAN AMERICAN CHAMBER OF COMMERCE

10350 Santa Monica Blvd, Ste 210
Los Angeles, CA 90025

(310) 557-3017
www.IACCW.net

ITALIAN AMERICAN CHAMBER OF COMMERCE

1800 W. Loop South, Suite 1120
Houston, TX 77027

(713) 626-9303
www.IACCTexas.com

ITALIAN CHAMBER OF COMMERCE IN CANADA

Suite 510, 789 W. Pender Street
Vancouver, BC V6C 1H2

(604) 682-1410
www.ICCBC.com

ITALIAN EMBASSY –
CONSULAR SECTION

3000 Whitehaven Street, N.W.
Washington, DC 20008

(202) 612-4400
www.ItalyEMB.org

ITALIAN VICE CONSULATE

One Gateway Center, Suite 100
Newark, NJ 07102

(973) 643-4716

ITALIAN CONSULATE
GENERAL

500 N. Michigan Ave., Ste 1850
Chicago, IL 60611

(312) 467-1550
www.ItalianConsChicago.org

ITALIAN CONSULATE
GENERAL

1300 Post Oak Blvd., Suite 660
Houston, TX 77056

(713) 850-7520
www.ItalianConsHouston.org

ITALIAN CONSULATE
GENERAL

12400 Wilshire Blvd. Suite 300
Los Angeles, CA 90025

(310) 820-0622
sedi.esteri.it/losangeles

ITALIAN CONSULATE
GENERAL

4000 Ponce de Leon, Suite 590
Coral Gables, FL 33146

(305) 374-6322
www.ItalConsMiami.com

> **ITALIAN CONSULATE GENERAL**

690 Park Avenue
New York, NY 10021

(212) 737-9100
www.ItalConsNYC.org

> **ITALIAN CONSULATE GENERAL**

1026 Public Ledger, 100 S. 6th St.
Philadelphia, PA 19106

(215) 592-7329
www.ItalConPhila.org

> **ITALIAN CONSULATE GENERAL**

2590 Webster Street
San Francisco, CA 94115

(415) 292-9210
www.ItalCons-SF.org

> **ITALIAN CONSULATE**

Buhl Building
535 Griswold Street, Suite 1840
Detroit, MI 48226

(313) 963-8560
www.ItalConsDetroit.org

This book can be purchased online at
www.UltimateItalianTrivia.com

APPENDIX B: LIST OF ITALIAN STATESMEN

KINGDOM OF ITALY (KINGS):
1861 – 1878 Victor Emmanuel II
1878 – 1900 Umberto I
1900 – 1946 Victor Emmanuel III
1946 Umberto II (Regent from 1944)

PRIME MINISTERS:
1861 Camillo Benso, Conte de Cavour
1861 – 1862 Bettino Ricàsoli
1862 Urbano Rattazzi
1862 – 1863 Luigi Carlo Farini
1863 – 1864 Marco Minghetti
1964 – 1866 Alfonso Ferrero, Cavaliere La-Màrmora
1866 – 1867 Bettino Ricàsoli (2nd term)
1867 – 1867 Urbano Rattazzi (2nd term)
1867 – 1869 Federico Luigi, Conte Menabrea
1869 – 1873 Giovanni Lanza
1873 – 1876 Marco Minghetti (2nd term)
1876 – 1878 Agostino Depretis
1878 Benedetto Càiroli
1878 – 1879 Agostino Depretis (2nd term)
1879 – 1881 Benedetto Càiroli (2nd term)
1881 – 1887 Agostino Depretis (3rd term)

1887 – 1891 Francesco Crispi
1891 – 1892 Antonio Starabba, Marchese di Rudinì
1892 – 1893 Giovanni Giolitti
1893 – 1896 Francesco Crispi (2nd term)
1896 – 1898 Antonio Starabba, Marchese di Rudinì (2nd term)
1898 – 1900 Luigi Pelloux
1900 – 1901 Giuseppe Saracco
1901 – 1903 Giuseppe Zanardelli
1903 – 1905 Giovanni Giolitti (2nd term)
1905 – 1906 Alessandro Fortis
1906 Sidney Sonnino
1906 – 1909 Giovanni Giolitti (3rd term)
1909 – 1910 Sidney Sonnino (2nd term)
1910 – 1911 Luigi Luzzatti
1911 – 1914 Giovanni Giolitti (4th term)
1914 – 1916 Antonio Salandra
1916 – 1917 Paolo Boselli
1917 – 1919 Vittorio Emanuele Orlando
1945 Ferruccio Parri
1945 – 1953 Alcide De Gasperi
1953 – 1954 Giuseppe Pella
1954 Amintore Fanfani
1954 – 1955 Mario Scelba
1955 – 1957 Antonio Segni
1957 – 1958 Adone Zoli
1958 – 1959 Amintore Fanfani (2nd term)
1959 – 1960 Antonio Segni (2nd term)

1960	Fernando Tambroni-Armaroli
1960 – 1963	Amintore Fanfani (3rd term)
1963	Giovanni Leone
1963 – 1968	Aldo Moro
1968	Giovanni Leone (2nd term)
1968 – 1970	Mariano Rumor
1970 – 1972	Emilio Colombo
1972 – 1973	Giulio Andreotti
1973 – 1974	Mariano Rumor (2nd term)
1974 – 1976	Aldo Moro (2nd term)
1976 – 1979	Giulio Andreotti (2nd term)
1979 – 1980	Francesco Cossiga
1980 – 1981	Arnaldo Forlani
1981 – 1982	Giovanni Spadolini
1982 – 1983	Amintore Fanfani (4th term)
1983 – 1987	Bettino Craxi
1987	Amintore Fanfani (5th term)
1987 – 1988	Giovanni Goria
1988 – 1989	Ciriaco De Mita
1989 – 1992	Giulio Andreotti (3rd term)
1992 – 1993	Giuliano Amato
1993 – 1994	Carlo Azeglio Ciampi
1994 – 1995	Silvio Berlusconi
1995 – 1996	Lamberto Dini
1996 – 1998	Romano Prodi
1998 – 2000	Massimo D'Alema
2000 – 2001	Giuliano Amato (2nd term)
2001 – 2006	Silvio Berlusconi (2nd term)
2006 +	Romano Prodi (2nd term)

REPUBLIC OF ITALY (PRESIDENTS):

1946 – 1948	Enrico da Nicola (Provisional Head of State)
1948 – 1955	Luigi Einaudi
1955 – 1962	Giovanni Gronchi
1962 – 1964	Antonio Segni
1964 – 1971	Giuseppe Saragat
1971 – 1978	Giovanni Leone
1978 – 1985	Sandro Pertini
1985 – 1992	Francesco Cossiga
1992 – 1999	Oscar Luigi Scalfaro
1999 – 2006	Carlo Azeglio Ciampi
2006 +	Giorgio Napolitano

L'INNO DI MAMELI

Fratelli d'Italia	Italian brothers,
L'Italia s'è desta	Italy has arisen,
Dell'elmo di Scipio	With Scipio's helmet
S'è cinta la testa.	binding her head.
Dove'è la Vittoria?.	Where is Victory?
Le porga la chioma;	Let her bow down,
Chè schiava di Roma	For God has made her
Iddio la creò.	The slave of Rome.
Stringiamoci a coorte,	Let us gather in legions,
Siam pronti alla morte:	Ready to die!
Italia chiamò!	Italy has called!
Noi siamo da secoli	We for centuries
Calpesti e derisi,	Have been downtrodden and derided,
Perchè non siam popolo,	Because we are not a people,
Perchè siam divisi;	Because we are divided.
Raccolgaci un'unica	Let one flag, one hope
Bandiera, un speme;	Bring us together;
Di fonderci insieme;	The hour has struck
Già l'ora suonò.	For us to join forces.
Stringiamoci a coorte,	Let us gather in legions,
Siam pronti alla morte:	Ready to die!
Italia chiamò!	Italy has called!
Uniamoci, amiamoci;	Let us unite and love one another;
L'unione e l'amore	For union and love
Rivelano ai popoli	Reveal to peoples
Le vie del Signore:	The way of the Lord
Giuriamo far libero	Let us swear to free

Il suolo natío;
Uniti per Dio
Chi vincer ci può?.
Stringiamoci a coorte,
Siam pronti alla morte:
Italia chiamò!

Dall'Alpi a Sicilia
Dovunque è Legnano
Ogni uom di Ferruccio:
Ha il cuor e la mano.
I bimbi d'Italia
Si chiamano Balilla:
Il suon d'ogni squilla
I vespri suonò.
Stringiamoci a coorte,
Siam pronti alla morte:
Italia chiamò!

Son giunchi che piegano
Le spade vendute
Già l'Aquila d'Austria:
Le penne ha perdute.
Il sangue d'Italia
E il sangue polacco
Bevè col Cosacco
Ma il cor le bruciò
Stringiamoci a coorte
Siam pronti alla morte:
Italia chiamò!

Our native soil;
If we are united under God,
Who can conquer us?
Let us gather in legions,
Ready to die!
Italy has called!

From the Alps to Sicily,
Everywhere it is Legnano;
Every man has the heart
and hand of Ferruccio.
The children of Italy
Are all called Balilla;
Every trumpet blast
Sounds the (Sicilian) Vespers.
Let us gather in legions,
Ready to die!
Italy has called!

Mercenary swords
Are feeble reeds,
And the Austrian eagle
Has lost his plumes.
This eagle that drunk the blood
of Italy and Poland,
together with the Cossack,
But this has burned his gut.
Let us gather in legions,
Ready to die!
Italy has called!

APPENDIX D: REGION PROFILES

Abruzzo

- ► **Capital:** L'Aquila
- ► **Municipalities:** 305
- ► **Population:** 1,305,307
  - Rank: 14th (2.2%)
  - Density: 118/km²
  - Growth Rate: 0.46%
- ► **Area:** 10,794 km²
  - Rank: 13th (3.6%)
- ► **Provinces:** 4   ► **Geography:**
  - Chieti   - Mountain: 65%
  - L'Aquila   - Lowland: 0%
  - Pescara   - Hill: 35%
  - Teramo

Aosta Valley (Valle d'Aosta)

- ► **Capital:** Aosta
- ► **Municipalities:** 74
- ► **Population:** 123,978
  - Rank: 20th (0.2%)
  - Density: 37/km²
  - Growth Rate: 0.90%
- ► **Area:** 3,263 km²
  - Rank: 20th (1.1%)
- ► **Provinces:** 1   ► **Geography:**
  - Aosta   - Mountain: 100%
                     - Lowland: 0%
                     - Hill: 0%

Apulia (Puglia)

- ► **Capital:** Bari
- ► **Municipalities:** 258
- ► **Population:** 4,071,518
  - Rank: 8th (7.1%)
  - Density: 208/km²
  - Growth Rate: 0.08%
- ► **Area:** 19,366 km²
  - Rank: 7th (6.4%)
- ► **Provinces:** 5   ► **Geography:**
  - Bari   - Mountain: 2%
  - Brindisi   - Lowland: 53%
  - Foggia   - Hill: 45%
  - Lecce
  - Taranto

Basilicata

- ► **Capital:** Potenza
- ► **Municipalities:** 131
- ► **Population:** 594,086
  - Rank: 18th (1.0%)
  - Density: 60/km²
  - Growth Rate: -0.41%
- ► **Area:** 9,995 km²
  - Rank: 14th (3.3%)
- ► **Provinces:** 2   ► **Geography:**
  - Matera   - Mountain: 47%
  - Potenza   - Lowland: 8%
                     - Hill: 45%

Calabria

- ▶ **Capital:** Catanzaro
- ▶ **Municipalities:** 409
- ▶ **Population:** 2,004,415
  - Rank: 10th (3.5%)
  - Density: 133/km²
  - Growth Rate: -0.24%
- ▶ **Area:** 15,081 km²
  - Rank: 10th (5.0%)
- ▶ **Provinces:** 5   ▶ **Geography:**
  - Catanzaro
  - Cosenza
  - Crotone
  - Reggio di
  - Vibo Valentia

- Mountain:	42%
- Lowland:	9%
- Hill:	49%

Campania

- ▶ **Capital:** Naples
- ▶ **Municipalities:** 551
- ▶ **Population:** 5,790,929
  - Rank: 2nd (10.0%)
  - Density: 426/km²
  - Growth Rate: 0.03%
- ▶ **Area:** 13,590 km²
  - Rank: 12th (4.5%)
- ▶ **Provinces:** 5   ▶ **Geography:**
  - Avellino
  - Benevento
  - Caserta
  - Naples
  - Salerno

- Mountain:	34%
- Lowland:	15%
- Hill:	51%

Emilia-Romagna

- ▶ **Capital:** Bologna
- ▶ **Municipalities:** 341
- ▶ **Population:** 4,187,557
  - Rank: 7th (7.0%)
  - Density: 189/km²
  - Growth Rate: 0.87%
- ▶ **Area:** 22,123 km²
  - Rank: 6th (7.3%)
- ▶ **Provinces:** 9   ▶ **Geography:**
  - Bologna
  - Ferrara
  - Forti-Cesena
  - Modena
  - Parma
  - Piacenza   - Reggio-Emilia
  - Ravenna   - Rimini

- Mountain:	25%
- Lowland:	48%
- Hill:	27%

Friuli-Venezia Giulia

- ▶ **Capital:** Trieste
- ▶ **Municipalities:** 219
- ▶ **Population:** 1,208,278
  - Rank: 15th (2.1%)
  - Density: 154/km²
  - Growth Rate: 0.30%
- ▶ **Area:** 7,856 km²
  - Rank: 17th (2.6%)
- ▶ **Provinces:** 4   ▶ **Geography:**
  - Gorizia
  - Pordenone
  - Trieste
  - Udine

- Mountain:	43%
- Lowland:	38%
- Hill:	19%

Latium (Lazio)

- ▶ **Capital:** Rome
- ▶ **Municipalities:** 377
- ▶ **Population:** 5,304,778
  - - Rank: 3rd (9.0%)
  - - Density: 308/km²
  - - Growth Rate: 0.66%
- ▶ **Area:** 17,208 km²
  - - Rank: 9th (5.7%)
- ▶ **Provinces:** 5
  - - Frosinone
  - - Latina
  - - Rieti
  - - Rome
  - - Viterbo

▶ **Geography:**
- - Mountain: 26%
- - Lowland: 20%
- - Hill: 54%

Liguria

- ▶ **Capital:** Genoa
- ▶ **Municipalities:** 235
- ▶ **Population:** 1,610,134
  - - Rank: 12th (2.8%)
  - - Density: 297/km²
  - - Growth Rate: 1.12%
- ▶ **Area:** 5,420 km²
  - - Rank: 18th (1.8%)
- ▶ **Provinces:** 4
  - - Genoa
  - - Imperia
  - - La Spezia
  - - Savona

▶ **Geography:**
- - Mountain: 65%
- - Lowland: 0%
- - Hill: 35%

Lombardy (Lombardia)

- ▶ **Capital:** Milan
- ▶ **Municipalities:** 1,546
- ▶ **Population:** 9,475,202
  - - Rank: 1st (15.8%)
  - - Density: 397/km²
  - - Growth Rate: 0.87%
- ▶ **Area:** 23,856 km²
  - - Rank: 4th (7.9%)
- ▶ **Provinces:** 11
  - - Bergamo
  - - Brescia
  - - Como
  - - Cremona
  - - Lecco
  - - Lodi
  - - Mantua

▶ **Geography:**
- - Mountain: 41%
- - Lowland: 12%
- - Hill: 47%

- - Milano
- - Monza e Brianza
- - Pavia

Marches (Marche)

- ▶ **Capital:** Ancona
- ▶ **Municipalities:** 246
- ▶ **Population:** 1,528,809
  - - Rank: 13th (2.6%)
  - - Density: 158/km²
  - - Growth Rate: 0.66%
- ▶ **Area:** 9,694 km²
  - - Rank: 15th (3.2%)
- ▶ **Provinces:** 5
  - - Ancona
  - - Ascoli Piceno
  - - Fermo
  - - Macerata
  - - Pesaro e Urbino

▶ **Geography:**
- - Mountain: 31%
- - Lowland: 0%
- - Hill: 69%

Molise

- ► **Capital:** Campobass
- ► **Municipalities:** 136
- ► **Population:** 320,907
  - Rank: 19th (0.6%)
  - Density: 72/km²
  - Growth Rate: -0.32%
- ► **Area:** 4,438 km²
  - Rank: 19th (1.5%)
- ► **Provinces:** 2
  - Campobasso
  - Isernia

► **Geography:**
  - Mountain: 55%
  - Lowland: 0%
  - Hill: 45%

Piedmont (Piedmonte)

- ► **Capital:** Turin
- ► **Municipalities:** 1,206
- ► **Population:** 4,341,733
  - Rank: 6th (7.4%)
  - Density: 167/km²
  - Growth Rate: 0.27%
- ► **Area:** 25,399 km²
  - Rank: 2nd (8.4%)
- ► **Provinces:** 8
  - Alessandria
  - Asti
  - Biella
  - Cuneo
  - Novara
  - Turin

► **Geography:**
  - Mountain: 43%
  - Lowland: 27%
  - Hill: 30%

  - Verbano-Cusio-Ossola
  - Vercelli

Sardinia (Sardegna)

- ► **Capital:** Cagliari
- ► **Municipalities:** 377
- ► **Population:** 1,655,677
  - Rank: 11th (2.9%)
  - Density: 69/km²
  - Growth Rate: 0.34%
- ► **Area:** 24,090 km²
  - Rank: 3rd (8.0%)
- ► **Provinces:** 4
  - Cagliari
  - Oristano
  - Sassari
  - Nuoro

► **Geography:**
  - Mountain: 14%
  - Lowland: 18%
  - Hill: 68%

Sicily (Sicilia)

- ► **Capital:** Palermo
- ► **Municipalities:** 390
- ► **Population:** 5,017,212
  - Rank: 4th (8.7%)
  - Density: 195/km²
  - Growth Rate: 0.08%
- ► **Area:** 25,708 km²
  - Rank: 1st (8.5%)
- ► **Provinces:** 9
  - Agrigento
  - Caltanisetta
  - Catania
  - Enna
  - Messina
  - Palermo
  - Ragusa

► **Geography:**
  - Mountain: 24%
  - Lowland: 14%
  - Hill: 62%

  - Syracuse
  - Trapani

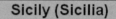

Trentino-Alto Adige

- ▶ **Capital:** Trento
- ▶ **Municipalities:** 339
- ▶ **Population:** 985,128
  - - Rank: 16th (1.6%)
  - - Density: 73/km²
  - - Growth Rate: 1.08%
- ▶ **Area:** 13,607 km²
  - - Rank: 11th (4.5%)
- ▶ **Provinces:** 2   ▶ **Geography:**
  - - Bolzano   - Mountain: 99%
  - - Trento   - Lowland: 0%
  -                  - Hill: 1%

Umbria

- ▶ **Capital:** Perugia
- ▶ **Municipalities:** 92
- ▶ **Population:** 867,878
  - - Rank: 17th (1.4%)
  - - Density: 103/km²
  - - Growth Rate: 1.04%
- ▶ **Area:** 8,456 km²
  - - Rank: 16th (2.8%)
- ▶ **Provinces:** 2   ▶ **Geography:**
  - - Perugia   - Mountain: 29%
  - - Terni   - Lowland: 0%
  -                  - Hill: 71%

Tuscany (Toscana)

- ▶ **Capital:** Florence
- ▶ **Municipalities:** 287
- ▶ **Population:** 3,619,872
  - - Rank: 9th (6.1%)
  - - Density: 158/km²
  - - Growth Rate: 0.60%
- ▶ **Area:** 22,990 km²
  - - Rank: 5th (7.6%)
- ▶ **Provinces:** 10   ▶ **Geography:**
  - - Arezzo   - Mountain: 25%
  - - Firenze   - Lowland: 8%
  - - Grosseto   - Hill: 67%
  - - Livorno
  - - Lucca   - Pistoia
  - - Massa-Carrara - Prato
  - - Pisa   - Siena

Veneto

- ▶ **Capital:** Venice
- ▶ **Municipalities:** 581
- ▶ **Population:** 4,738,313
  - - Rank: 5th (7.9%)
  - - Density: 249/km²
  - - Growth Rate: 0.82%
- ▶ **Area:** 18,391 km²
  - - Rank: 8th (6.1%)
- ▶ **Provinces:** 7   ▶ **Geography:**
  - - Belluno   - Mountain: 29%
  - - Padova   - Lowland: 56%
  - - Rovigo   - Hill: 15%
  - - Treviso
  - - Venezia
  - - Verona   - Vicenza

BIBLIOGRAPHY

❖ BARONE, Artuo, *Italians First*. Kent, U.K.: Renaissance Books, 1999

❖ BELLO, Nino, The *Incredible Book of Vatican Facts and Papal Curiosities*. New York: Barnes & Noble Books, 1998

❖ BUNYON, Patrick, *All Around the Town*. New York: Fordham University Press, 1999

❖ BURCKHARDT, Jacob, *The Civilization of the Renaissance in Italy*. New York: Harper Torchbooks of Harper & Row, 1958

❖ CAOATTI, Alberto & MONTANARI, Massimo, *Italian Cuisine*. New York: Columbia University Press, 2003

❖ CIPOLLA, GAETANO, *What Italy Has Given to the World*. Mineola, New York: Legas, 1994

❖ CLARK, Martin, *Modern Italy 1871-1982*. New York: Longman Publishing Group, 1996

❖ DUGGAN, Christopher, *A Concise History of Italy*. Cambridge, U.K.: Cambridge University Press, 1994

❖ ESPIRO, Peter and Pinkowish, Mary, *Sprezzatura*. New York: Anchor Books, 2001

❖ ESPOSITO, Russell, *The Golden Milestone*. New York: The New York Learning Library, 2000

❖ EUVINO, Gabrielle and Filippo, Michael San, *The Complete Idiot's Guide to Italian History and Culture*. Indianapolis: Penguin Group, 2002

❖ GRUN, Bernard, *The Timetables of History*. New York: Touchstone of Simon and Schuster, 1982

❖ HIRSCH, Kett and Trefil, *The Dictionary of Cultural Literacy*. Boston: Houghton Mifflin Company, 1988

❖ HOLMES, George, *The Oxford Illustrated History of Italy*. Oxford, U.K.: Oxford University Press, 2001

❖ KEATES, Jonathan, *The Rouge Guide History of Italy*. London: Penguin Group, 2003

❖ LINTNER, Valerio, *A Traveler's History of Italy*. Northampton: Interlink Books, 2004

❖ MARIANI, John, *The Dictionary of Italian Food and Drink*. New York: Broadway Books, 1998

❖ MONTAGU, John, *Battles of the Greek & Roman Worlds*. London: Greenhill Books, 2000

❖ OUR SUNDAY'S VISITOR, *2005 Catholic Almanac*. Huntington, IN: Our Sunday Visitor, 2005

❖ MESSADIE, Gerald, *Great Scientific Discoveries*. New York: Chambers, 1991

❖ MESSADIE, Gerald, *Great Inventions Through History*. New York: Chambers, 1991

❖ OXFORD, *Oxford Dictionary of Quotations*. Oxford: Oxford University Press, 1980

❖ PESCOSOLIDO, Carl, and Gleason, Pamela. *The Proud Italians*. Washington: Latium Publishing, distributed by the National Italian-American Foundation, 1991

❖ RADOMILE, Leon J., *Heritage Italian-American Style*. Novato, California. Vincero Enterprises, 1999

❖ RODGERS, Nigel, *The History and Conquests of Ancient Rome*. London: Anness Publishing, 2005

❖ ROOT, Waverly, *The Food of Italy*. New York: Vintage Books, 1971

❖ SCARRE, Chris, *Smithsonian Timelines of the Ancient World*. London: Dorling Kindersley, 1993

❖ SPIGNESI, Stephen, *The Italian 100*. New York: Citadel Press Books, 2003

INDEX

www.ItalianTrivia.com

Looking for Italian trivia online? Your search is over. Italian trivia online can be found be visiting www.ItalianTrivia.com. There you will find some of the same great trivia from this book, plus newly added trivia from readers and trivia buffs alike. New trivia is added monthly.

This website also provides links to many outstanding Italian organizations and publications dedicated to the Italian heritage.

FEEDBACK ENCOURAGED

Readers of *Ultimate Italian Trivia* are highly encouraged to provide feedback to the author. Please feel free to write or email your thoughts, questions or comments. In addition, please feel free to send suggestions or provide new trivia for future editions of this book. Select endorsements will be considered for placement in a special section of this book for future printings and editions. Please use the following contact information:

Mailing Address: Marshall Rand Publishing
P.O. Box 1849
Royal Oak, MI 48068-1849

Email: Contact@MarshallRand.com

ORDER FORM

The Perfect Christmas and Birthday Gift

Internet Orders: www.Amazon.com **or** www.ScottPaulFrush.com

Fax Orders: (248) 232-1501 (credit card only – please include this form)

Postal Orders: Marshall Rand Publishing
P.O. Box 1849
Royal Oak, MI 48068-1849

Ship to:

Name:_____

Address:_____

City:_____ State:_____ Zip:_____

Telephone:_____

Item:

Book: ***Ultimate Italian Trivia*** $ 14.75
        A Treasure Trove of Fun and Fascinating Facts

Postage: 1.00

Sales Tax: (Michigan residents, add $0.89 for each book)   _____

Total: (please sum) $_____

Payment: ☐ Check   ☐ Visa   ☐ MasterCard

Please make check payable to *Marshall Rand Publishing*

Card number:_____

Name on card:_____ Exp. Date:_____